Shed bash
The Bea

G000229856

A Trainspotter in the Swinging Sixties

Phil Mathison

Published by Dead Good Publications
Newport
East Yorkshire
HU15 2RF

Warning

Incidentally, trespassing on railway property was, and is, a criminal offence, besides being extremely dangerous. As a responsible publisher, I cannot condone or encourage such activities. The narrative within these pages is the account of one individual's experiences in his youth, and should in no way be emulated. Do not put yourself at risk of injury, death or prosecution in the pursuit of your interests.

ISBN 0-9546937-3-6

Published by Dead Good Publications
Newport
East Yorkshire
HU15 2RF

©2006

Contents

Chapter 1   Young Hopefuls storm Cop Charts   5

Chapter 2   Fab Four Fan Club   12

Chapter 3   It won't be long (until the next train trip!)   18

Chapter 4   A solo career   25

Chapter 5   You really got me!   30

Chapter 6   I feel fine   36

Chapter 7   Eight days a week   41

Chapter 8   Ticket to ride   47

Chapter 9   Help!   52

Chapter 10 Satisfaction   58

Chapter 11 Yesterday   64

Chapter 12 Day Tripper   69

Chapter 13 You won't see me   75

Chapter 14 Nineteenth nervous breakdown   81

Chapter 15 Run for your life   86

Chapter 16 Paperback Writer   92

Chapter 17 Here, there and everywhere   97

Chapter 18 I want to tell you   102

Chapter 19 Friday on my mind   109

Chapter 20 I'm a believer   114

Chapter 21 I can hear the grass grow   119

Chapter 22 A day in the life (of a shed basher)   125

Chapter 23 Hello, goodbye   133

Introduction

Like many others, I'm the last of a generation. The generation that remembers steam, real steam, the way it actually was in the final years of operation on British Railways in the Sixties. I was one of those insane individuals who risked life and limb, pouring all our energies into chasing those elusive numbers. We spent our last penny in pursuit of a sighting that meant another conquest. The reward for all our heroic efforts? A thin blue, or red, or black line underscoring a number in our abc spotter's book. Such effort, for so slight a prize. and yet..... Looking back from a more prosaic age, such endeavours seem disproportionate, in fact, bordering on the ridiculous, but in the Sixties, the chase was for real. Steam traction was disappearing fast, and like thousands of others, I tracked down those valuable cops with the dedication of a big game hunter. Only when steam died in August 1968 did I put the abc book, the timetables and the notebook away.

I'd like to acknowledge the help of several people, without whose assistance this book wouldn't have been possible. My mother, who passed away in 1997, was very patient, for I pestered the life out of her to go on so many trips. As my father was at sea most of the time that my adventures took place, it fell to her to pack me up, and make sure that I got off in a presentable fashion, even at five in the morning. She'd then worry about me all day, and would always be up when I arrived home, no matter what the hour was. Next, I'd like to thank my long suffering wife, Mary, for her patience, especially in proof reading text that must have bored her senseless. The book mentions a number of enthusiasts who were close trainspotting confidants. There was Dave, who was very patient with a lad three years his junior. I last saw him at Christmas 1967, and I wish him well wherever he is now. Next, there was my school friend Brian, with whom I spent many happy days spotting around Hull between 1962 and 1968. Then there was Ian, who introduced me to travel further afield in 1963, and accompanied me on a number of trips in the Sixties. Last, but by no means least, is Mike, five years my senior, who was already an old hand at the spotting game in February 1964, when I accompanied him on the first of no less than 42 trips together. Finally, I'd like to mention the hundreds of spotters that I met on my travels. There was a great camaraderie among the shed bashing fraternity, and I hope that if you were one of them, you remember those days with as much fondness as I do.

Chapter 1

Young Hopefuls storm Cop Charts

It was April 1969, eight months after steam had finished on B.R., and during a tea break from work at the greenhouses in Brough, I watched three forlorn ex-L.M.S. engines being towed past by a Brush type 4 diesel. They were probably the last batch bound for Draper's scrap yard in Hull; the end of an era. With a sigh in my heart and 'Get Back' by The Beatles playing on the radio, my mind ran back over six years to the first time that I'd heard the 'Fab Four'. It was late 1962, and I had just been initiated into the Secret Society of Serial Shed Bashers. Yes, I'd like to 'get back', back to the chase, back to the thrill of new places, and on the trail of new cops, and most of all, back to that 'other' world, the one that was steam powered.

Hull Dairycoates, my local shed, had given me my first taste of shed bashing in the summer of 1962. It was a vast depot, sitting in the middle of a triangle of lines. On the north eastern side, there was the branch from the docks in East Hull to Neptune Street. To the south there were the direct lines from the docks in West Hull to Outward Yard, and to the north west, there was the main line, on an embankment, to Leeds and Doncaster. My earliest memories are of marching past the diesel depot and a line of stored J72s, 69009, 69010, 69011, and 69020, which were waiting to be transferred away. By the winter, I'd become addicted to the ways of the trainspotter, and was in time to observe the last K3 2-6-0s and J39 0-6-0s being withdrawn. I'd watched them working hard all the previous summer, but did not realise how close they were to oblivion. I remember one K3, 61906 I believe, in steam at the turntable at the west end of the roundhouse in the worst of the January 1963 snows, but its reprieve was short. A sad line had already formed on '7' section, waiting for their final journey. An unusual bedfellow with them was 'Jinty' 47556, which amazingly outlasted them by many months. The first time I saw The Beatles they were performing on the T.V. programme 'Scene at 6-30', playing 'Love me do'. Another skiffle group that won't last ten minutes, I thought to myself. How wrong can one be!

I had only just turned eleven at the beginning of 1963, but I wanted to travel anywhere there was steam, so I pestered my mother relentlessly to 'Please, Please Me', and let me go to York on my own, just to spot on the station of course. I first went there in April, and took up my position with the gaggle of other spotters at the north end of the island platform. What I remember to this day is the thrill of hearing a chime whistle sound opposite York depot, and then a few moments later, one of Gresley's finest coasting round the curve and into the station. I can't remember what my first A4 was, for the notes from these early trips have not survived, but I did cop ten of the beasts at York that year. I kept my promise not to trespass until June, but then the temptation was just too great, and York South shed became my first 'away' conquest. Stored on shed were 40117, 41251, 41265, 46473, 60831, 60837, 60154, 65844, 65888, 65894, 82027 and 82028. Some were to work again, but some were not. Spurred on by this triumph, and with my friend Brian's bravado to bolster me, York North shed fell the next month. Our eyes popped out when 9F 92231 welcomed us at the entrance, for our locoshed books had it allocated to 71A Eastleigh! We hadn't realised that it had just been transferred north. I made four more trips to York during the summer, the last one on September 28th. By way of variation, I made a trip to Doncaster on August 15th, with a fellow spotter, Dave. He was one of a nucleus of regulars who gathered at Anlaby Road crossings, particularly for the 7.22 pm arrival from Kings Cross. Unusually, he lived some distance away, down Dundee Street, off Perth Street, but the other regulars, such as Ian and Mike, of whom you will hear more in due time, both lived off the Boulevard. Dave, at fourteen, was older than me, but we struck up a good friendship that was to last until he left Riley High School in 1967. Unfortunately, he advised against bashing Doncaster shed, because of its fearsome shedmaster. Temptingly, we walked along the perimeter fence; so near and yet so far from all those L.N.E.R. beauties! However, his nerve didn't fail him when he wanted to go out with my sister, Joan! Still, I count myself fortunate to have seen many of the A1s, A3s, A4s and V2s still in service on that very last 'Indian Summer' of East Coast Main Line steam in 1963, and all for the cost of a half price day return at five shillings and thru'pence. Living down St. Matthew Street, it was hardly surprising that trainspotting should become my hobby, for our street was halfway between the goods lines at the end of South Boulevard, and Anlaby Road crossings to the north. You could always hear the sound of buffers clanging when you came out of the house. I started the summer as a pupil at Constable Street Primary School, but I was to follow in Dave's footsteps, and become a pupil at Riley High School by its end.

The Beatles visited Hull twice in 1963, the first time when they had only just started their meteoric rise to the top. They played at The Majestic, and while driving their van back home, George Harrison drove off the road at Goole, and was fined for careless driving at Goole Magistrates' Court! By the time that they returned to the city on November 24th, they were huge celebrities and filled the ABC Theatre full to overflowing. By the close of the year, the band were undisputed champions of the British pop scene, and 'Jinty' 47556 had finally disappeared from the scrapline at Hull Dairycoates. However, the Liverpudlian group were not the only ones enjoying success. In the month that they visited Hull for the second time I visited Darlington shed and works with the local trainspotting society. What a revelation! The shed had all the usual suspects - Q6s, J27s, B1s, K1s, and no less than 11 J94s. Highlights on shed to me were always the 'scrappers' lurking out of the way, and Darlington shed did not disappoint - V3 67652, WD 2-10-0 90751 and 'Clans' 72001 and 72002, then only a few years old. Nothing could prepare me for the works though. Even now, after forty years, I cannot forget the sight that met me that sunny autumn afternoon, as I walked towards the scrapyard. It was like a graveyard, with trees growing up through the track, and all around locomotives in every state of disembowelment! L1 67755 and T1 69921 were already too far gone to be counted as 'cops' (The old 'when is a cop not a cop argument!'), but Clans 72000 & 72003 weren't. Also present were ex-Scottish region V3s 67607, 67618, 67632, 67635 and J50s 68892, 68937, 68965 and 68988, withdrawn from Ardsley and Copley Hill. Disappointingly, the main shops were home to a number of Sulzer Type 2s that were being built there, but the pen got busy again with A1s 60129 & 60139. Darlington had by then taken over the steam repairing duties of Derby and Doncaster, and so it was that Standard 5 4-6-0s 73048, 73092, 73130, 73162 and Standard 4s 75015 and 75049 were there. Thornaby was also visited that day, and even though it was not to shut to steam until December 1964, I only recorded 7 steam engines on shed, the most notable being V2s 60859 & 60946. As we waited in the dark for our train at York, a class 37 passed through on a southbound freight, with a wagon axlebox on fire. That raised a few eyebrows, and made for a talking point as we headed home after having a day full of fun exploring pastures new, and all for the total cost of twenty five shillings.

December 1963 saw The Beatles once again at number one with 'I want to hold your hand'. All I wanted to hold was my Locoshed book, Locoshed Directory, and a ticket to anywhere steam, but the shedmaster at Lincoln did want to hold my hand - but only to sling me out of there! All I saw were B1s 61006, 61058, 61348 and 61409, and then Ian and I made a hasty retreat. At Retford, I witnessed 11 O2s, recently withdrawn from the High Dyke iron ore trains waiting for scrap. I still didn't manage Doncaster shed, as Ian, a less hardy spirit, deemed it 'too dark' to visit. What frustration, for it was chock full of withdrawn East Coast super power, as well as more O2s! To this day, I regret that decision, but Ian was older, and had probably copped all his Gresley pacifics! Anyway, I wasn't going to argue, as a few days later, on the last Sunday before Christmas, I was to visit Manchester and Stockport with him. By this time, Hull was completely steam free on a Sunday, and so it was a great delight to arrive at Leeds City and see 61353, 42196, 63417, 42689 and 44803, very much in steam, on parcels, passenger and works trains. Ian soon had me trained to collect the numbers at motive power depots that we passed on the way, and so I was at the right vestibule window three times in quick succession as we passed Farnley, Mirfield and then Huddersfield, all in a twenty mile stretch after leaving Leeds. When we reached Manchester, we did Trafford Park first, then Agecroft. The latter shed housed Jubilee 45737, and 0F tank 47009, but otherwise all was standard fare. Stockport Edgeley was notable for 3 Jubilees, 45633, 45663 and 45732, the rest being mostly 'Black Fives' and 'Crabs'. Heaton Mersey seemed like '8F City', but it also held Jubilee 45569, a number of 'Coffee Pots' and a few 4Fs in its depths. So ended my first full year as a serial shed basher. A few triumphs, but like The Beatles, the best was yet to come!

1964 started out auspiciously, with a visit to Hull of a surprise celebrity from Liverpool. On January 4th, Brian and I were on Hessle Road flyover, trainspotting as usual, when a vision drifted down the embankment from Hessle, past Dairycoates depot and towards us. Surely it was a Royal Scot! But as it swept past us and under the flyover, we danced for joy at seeing Edge Hill Patriot 45531 'Sir Frederick Harrison'. It was bringing Everton football supporters to Hull on a special. In the event, the year was to be a big one for me and January was just the countdown, '5-4-3-2-1' as Manfred Mann sang, to a great spotting year, for I managed about 80 shed visits that year, excluding my local depot. So little time, so many sheds to do, so little pocket money! I may have lacked finance, but I had plenty of energy and ambition, and so was ultimately to be amply recompensed with experiences that are still in my memory bank.

The Beatles might not have been able to buy love that spring, but extra pocket money bought my love of steam for me, when I got my hands on a ticket for a special trip to Derby and Crewe sheds on April 18th. The special was hauled by A3 60051 'Blink Bonny' between the two towns, and what a treat that day was to be. I made more cops in that one day than I ever did before, or was to do afterwards, with a total of over 260 steam locomotives. Derby Works only held preserved 2-6-4T 42500. The shed was more promising, with Jubilees 45585, 45611, 45612, 45667, 45684 and 45742, and also 0F tank 47000. However, Derby was infested with 'Rats' of the worst kind - Sulzer Type 2 diesels. They were everywhere! So Crewe beckoned, that Mecca for any steam enthusiast. What an eye opener the town turned out to be in the eyes of this twelve year old! Crewe North shed furnished 12 Britannia pacifics and Patriots 45512, 45526 and 45534. However, the highlight had to be Coronations 46228, 46229, 46235, 46240, 46248 and 46251. Crewe South had over 70 locos on shed. Grange 4-6-0s 6803, 6817, 6819 and 6825 were on the depot, for Gresty Lane had just shut, and all ex G.W.R. engines were now serviced at the south shed. Strangely, no other class of G.W.R. locos were present, but Coronation 46243 and Jubilees 45558, 45567 and 45586 were noted. Leaving the best until last, Crewe Works was like a dream come true to this young spotter, for its hallowed walls contained 87 steam locomotives. After all these years, the numbers that leap off the page at me are G2a 0-8-0 49395, in for preservation, and Jubilee 4-6-0s 45569, 45626 and 45647. The site seemed so massive, with bits of engines everywhere, some for repair, but Crewe was also still scrapping even at that late stage. Memories are made of times like that fine April day all those years ago.

By the summer, I was getting to be a hardened traveller and spotter. Often leaving home at 06.00 or earlier, and never getting back before 21.00, I knew what The Beatles were singing about by the time they released 'A Hard Day's Night' on July 10th. With that song ringing in my ears, I set off the following day with my friend Barry, for my first visit to Carlisle and Dumfries, which was to be my first Scottish shed. Leeds Holbeck was my initial port of call, and from a visit the previous month, I knew the ropes. I was one of the 'Hole in the Wall' gang. There was a damaged wall at one end of the shed, and that was our means of entry. I wasn't thrown out that day, and amazingly, I never was thrown out of Holbeck shed, which is more than I can say for some sheds! There were 7 Jubilee 4-6-0s on shed that hot July morning, and one, 45620, was to haul my train that day. However, it disgraced itself, for it failed at Ais Gill. We limped into Carlisle Citadel 40 minutes late with the assistance of 'Black Five' 44682. The Beatles might have been off conquering the U.S.A., but that 40 minutes cost me my connection, and hence the opportunity to conquer my first Scottish shed. Such is fate! A brisk walk up Botchergate brought me to Upperby shed, and my first surprise of the day - Princess 4-6-2 46200, 'The Princess Royal' herself, in store. Other fine examples of ex-L.M.S. premier power were Patriots 45526, 45532 and 45545, Royal Scots 46110 and 46118, and Jubilees 45584, 45592, 45705, while 45640 passed as I jotted down the numbers. Cream of the Crop, naturally, were the Coronation pacifics - 46225, 46226, 46238 and 46250. I witnessed not one, but two more pass the shed during my visit - 46241 and 46254. What a magnificent sight they made as they stormed out of Carlisle, working out their last summer before the shortening days of autumn spelt the demise for all the remaining members of this marvellous class.

It seemed a long journey up Etterby Road to Kingmoor shed, but the 90 steam engines on shed made up for the stifling bus ride. I may have missed my first Scottish shed visit, but I was rewarded at Kingmoor with the sight of my first A2 pacifics - 60522 and 60524. Well, at least they were allocated to Scotland, the last Eastern and North Eastern region examples having been withdrawn immediately prior to my initial excursion to York! Further delights were Coronations 46255 and 46257, Royal Scots 46132, 46162 and 46166, and Clan 4-6-2 72005. Ex-L.N.E.R. locos present were A1 60118 and B1s 61308 and 61320. Also on shed were 8 Jubilee 4-6-0s and 5 Britannia 4-6-2s. Having been cruelly denied my incursion into Scottish territory by a recalcitrant steam loco, I had a little time on my hands, and so Barry and I settled down on the railway embankment near Kingmoor depot. To anyone unfamiliar with those days, it is very difficult to express the sheer delight of eating cucumber sandwiches under a summer sky, while watching regular and frequent steam services drift past your viewpoint. In the space of just half an hour, I recorded 70035, 43036, 44902, 45423, 43103, 73127, 70037, 70011, 45601, 60131, 44906 and 45635 run past! Sheer heaven, but fated to be just a memory within four short years, at which time I would sing along with The Rolling Stones 'It's all over now'. Time was indeed running out for what had once seemed a timeless spectacle.

Chapter 2

Fab Four Fan Club

Living in Hull, my early trainspotting days were naturally dominated by ex L.N.E.R. engines, with a few ex L.M.S. locos for variety. A regular spot for me was the footbridge at Anlaby Road crossings, for I used to go there most Saturday mornings, and then graduate to Dairycoates shed in the afternoon. I clearly remember my dad, who was a private hire taxi driver at the time, driving past and waving to me as I stood on the footbridge at the north side of Anlaby Road crossings. It's hard to imagine now, but he had a wholesale sweet rep as a regular client. Imagine that nowadays, a rep with no car! They were also hard times, for my dad has lost his job at sea in 1961. After a year as a shop keeper between 1961 and 1962, he'd lost nearly all his redundancy pay, and so he'd started taxi-ing in the bad winter of 1962/3. It nearly wrecked his car, a 1958 Vauxhall Victor that he'd bought in 1961, and so money was tight, very tight indeed. In fact, my parents sold all my Hornby three rail train set to buy me presents for Christmas 1963! What made it worse, was that I'd bought parts of it myself, including a beautiful reconditioned A4 locomotive that had cost me 34/6! However, this was no time to feel sorry for myself, for the pre Christmas 1963 trip to Manchester had broadened my horizons, both shed and region wise, and now I wanted more. 1964 arrived with no lines drawn under any of the numbers in either the ex S.R., or ex G.W.R. sections of my Ian Allan Combined Volume of British Railways Locomotives. This was to change on February 15th, when Hull City Football Club were to play Wrexham.

The night before, Ian asked me to join him on the cheap day excursion to be run for the match. Now, finance was always a source of major concern to me. The week before, The Beatles had released the 'All my Loving' EP, and to pursue all my loving (of steam engines), I needed 'Money', just like they were singing about. At only twelve, the twelve shillings and sixpence for the fare was a big deal, and so it really was a last minute scrounge that gathered the funds for this outing. The Americans may talk now about 'More Bangs for your Buck', but I looked at it then in the light of 'More Cops for your Coppers'! It was all about value for money, especially pre-decimal currency! Sixty two pence these days would scarcely buy a couple of Mars bars, but it was a small fortune to a twelve year old in 1964.

At 09.45 the next day, Ian and I met up with another spotting pal, Jim, and at 10.00 we were off into uncharted territory aboard a rattling D.M.U. In those days, any excursion from Hull towards Manchester went the Lancashire & Yorkshire route via Goole and Wakefield, to join the L.N.W.R. route at Thornhill Junction. An excursion from Constable Street Primary School had taken the same route to Belle Vue Zoo the previous summer, and that outing had given me a taste for spotting further afield, particularly when I saw so many ex L.M.S. engines, for they were not that common around Hull. Unfortunately, I have no records of the trip, only a tiny blurred photograph of a miniature steam engine at the zoo! While the masses on the coach were talking football, us three had our heads firmly out of the windows! Once past Manchester Exchange, I copped nearly everything I saw, but the best was yet to come.

Now, Jim, like me, had never seen a G.W.R. loco in the flesh, so to speak. No sooner had we pulled out of Chester station than a sight that I will never forget came into view. Green livery, polished brass rimmed chimney, and finally a nameplate - 'Burton Hall' confirmed beyond doubt that our first ever ex G.W.R. engine, Hall 6922, was in the cop bag! Jim and I danced around with excitement. The Beatles doing 'Twist and Shout' had nothing on us! We'd scarcely calmed down when Castle 7014 'Caerhays Castle' passed us, followed closely by Modified Hall 7916, 'Mobberley Hall'. We were over the moon, even before we had reached our destination. To see these wonderful locos, close up for the first time, just going about their everyday workings was one of the great thrills of my life. As I wondered at all those superb locomotives, the Fab Fours' album track 'You really got a hold on me' came to mind. The football fans may have had their obsession, but we had ours.

No sooner had the train stopped, than the football aficionados set off one way, and we were off in another direction to Croes Newydd shed. Formerly 89B, it was 6C by this time. I visited this depot on a number of occasions after this, and I always met with the same response - 'You've come all this way to look at our locos? Have a look round, but be careful now'. The railwaymen seemed genuinely amazed that young lads would travel from Yorkshire to spot a load of grimy freight engines. Grimy or not, these engines looked wonderful to me - Pannier 0-6-0Ts 1628, 1632, 1660, 3749, 3789, 4683, 7431 and 9669. 28xx 2-8-0s 3813, 3824 and 3829, and finally, 56xx 0-6-2Ts 6611, 6625 and 6651. There were a few others on shed, but I had now actually seen over a dozen ex G.W.R. locos!

We travelled on to Gobowen, where a push-pull service hauled by 2-6-2T 41285 took us to Oswestry. The little ex Cambrian Railway Locomotive Works was in its last days, and we really wanted to visit it before it closed. The welcome here was not so warm.
'Mister, can we look around the Works? We've come all the way from Hull.'
'I don't care where you've come from, sling your hook!' was the reply from the watchman on that Saturday afternoon.
Disappointed, but not discouraged, we moved on to the shed. It had a number of Ivatt 2-6-0s on, but the highlight for me had to be the Western stuff - 1438, 1638, 1668, 3208, 5421, Hall 6934, 7428, 7434, and last but not least, 7033 'Hartlebury Castle'.
We got back to Wrexham just in time for the return trip to Hull. We saw more ex G.W.R. engines on the way back, but it was soon too dark for much of 'the passing trade'. Jim and I sat down and counted up - we'd seen (and copped) THIRTY Western locos! We all agreed - what an absolutely FAB day out!

However, to be a full member of the Fab Four Fan Club, I needed to see locos from all four companies. Therefore, a visit to the Southern Region was required. London called, and on May 2nd, I answered. The local trainspotting society had organised a trip to Nine Elms, Feltham, Willesden and Watford. In the event, Watford was missed out due to late running. The lack of steam south of Peterborough made for a dismal hour or so on the journey down, but the grand entrance to Nine Elms more than made up for it. Southern steam super power at it's finest. No fewer than 15 Light Pacifics, and 8 Merchant Navy engines were on shed. I was now officially a member of the Fab Four Fan Club! There were also U and N 2-6-0s, and a solitary Q1, 33040. However, tucked away in the shed was a little gem - withdrawn M7 0-4-4T 30111. What it

14

was doing there, I don't know. It was obviously withdrawn, but my shed book had it down as allocated to Bournemouth. It was a delight to underline all these numbers in my Combined Volume, especially the Exmouth Junction based pacifics. If London was like the moon to me, Exeter might as well have been Mars!

It seemed a long way out to Feltham, and it was on this stretch that we lost time. It was worth if though, for it was the only occasion that I saw Class W 2-6-4Ts. Numbers 31912 / 13 / 14 / 17 and 31924 were present on shed that day. The depot also contained 8 S15 4-6-0s and 6 more Q1 0-6-0s. Willesden now beckoned, so we travelled from Southern super power to Midland super power. Willesden seemed a massive shed to me as a youngster. It was the only time that I had the opportunity to bash it, complete with 66 steam locos. No fewer than 10 Britannia Pacifics were on shed, along with Patriot 45530, and Jubilees 45617, 45652, 45676 and 45704. I had already seen a number of Coronations on other trips, but they never failed to impress me, some in red livery, some in green. Numbers 46239, 46240 and 46245 were in steam that day.

Now, some of the lads in the party were in the know, and they set off down the road to Old Oak Common. However, despite protests that we should try to gain entry, the trip organiser felt that a lack of a permit was a bit of a bar to that. Instead, the rest of us got paraded off for an hour's spotting on Paddington. It was a poor substitute by this date, as I only saw 4 pannier tanks, as all passenger trains were diesel hauled. It was a sad end to the day, as I never managed to bash Old Oak Common. One of life's regrets - we all have our 'might have beens'. It was a close run thing though, for the following week, I was in London again. It was a rugby league excursion this time, not a football one.

In April, Hull Kingston Rovers had defeated Oldham 12 : 2, and so they were off to Wembley on Saturday May 9th to challenge Widnes for the cup. Now, as I lived near the Hull F.C. ground, and my friends were Hull supporters, not H.K.R., you would have expected that we'd keep our gobs shut and enjoy the chance of a cheap trip down to 'The Smoke', with our heads out of the windows all the way! However, that wasn't Mike's way, for Hull's black and white strip was similar to Widnes's, and he couldn't resist wearing his black and white scarf on the train down. It was therefore no surprise that it got pinched off him on the way down! Nowadays, he'd have probably been thrown out of the window, but to show how different those days were, the scarf was returned to him when we reached London! It was not only a steamier age, but also a more civil one. We were as keen as mustard, even though the excursion set off from Hull at the ungodly hour of 04.30. The special followed the Great Central all the way from Sheffield. It was the only time that I travelled the whole of this marvellous route. In brilliant sunshine, (it always seemed to be sunny on those trips. Is that just memory playing tricks, or the rose coloured glasses of nostalgia?), we passed Annesley and Woodford Halse sheds. Apart from endless processions of O4 and O1 2-8-0s en route, the highlights were Patriot 45535, Royal Scot 46156 and Coronation 46251, seen on the West Coast main line at Rugby.

Before the train had even stopped at Marylebone Station, I was running, along with my friends Mike and Ian, down the platform to our first shed, 14A Cricklewood. There were 27 locos on shed, with V2s 60837 and 60923, along with Jubilees 45579 and 45694 being of note. Apart from Watford at the end of day, which we had missed the week before, the rest of the day was in Western Region territory, which suited me! Anyway, we first bashed 81C Southall, home to two Castles 5018 and 5041 and a wide range of ex G.W.R. motive power. Forlorn in one corner was King 6028, a poor shadow of its former self. A sad sight indeed at the start of the day. Next was 81B Slough, which was on the point of closure, and held just one loco - 6143. Then we were straight out to 81E Didcot. Of course we passed Reading on the way, but we were going to do that later in the day. Our eyes were firmly fixed to the left, on Reading (Southern), sub shed of Guildford. There were four Ns in steam - 31401, 31412, 31831 and 31862.

Apart from 2 9Fs, Didcot was all pure Western motive power. We had a little time there, and Mike, being ahead of his time not only possessed a colour cine camera, but also a portable tape recorder! When we'd done the shed, he decided to film a loco leaving the depot. He was in charge of the filming, and I was in charge of the taping. Good teamwork, spoiled by ecstatic utterances! I'd been called a chatterbox at primary school, and the inability to keep my mouth shut caused pained expressions from Mike on more than one occasion when recording! Next on the list was Oxford, 81F. This was a busy place, with over 40 on shed, mostly Halls and

Modified Halls, and two visiting ex L.M.S. 8F 2-8-0s 48345 and 48609. Our final shed on the Western was Reading 81D. Now, Castles were always a favourite of mine, and Reading depot didn't disappoint me, for it had 6 of the beasts on, and 4082 'Windsor Castle' passed as we went round. Two strangers in the camp were U 2-6-0 31800 and 4F 0-6-0 44334. With a clutch of Grange, Manor and Halls under our belts, we headed off to our last port of call - Watford. We passed Old Oak Common of course, but it was the only occasion that I saw the depot in steam days. The next time I passed, in April 1966, it was a wilderness from a steam perspective.

Watford was only a small depot, with just 10 locos on shed, mostly 'Coffee Pot' or Standard 2MT moguls. It was now well into the evening, and we all chatted away about the exploits of the day as we wearily made our way back to Marylebone Station for a departure just before midnight. I can't remember if Hull Kingston Rovers won that day. However, what I can remember, is 3 very happy youngsters stepping out onto Hull Paragon Station on Sunday morning at 04.30. I'd just copped 247 steam engines for a cost of thirty-seven shillings and eight pence. That worked out at just under two old pennies per cop. Good value, and I was now firmly a member of The Fab Four Fan Club! Just like The Beatles sang on the 'With The Beatles' album, I thought 'It won't be long' before my next trip, and it wasn't - just 7 days.

Chapter 3

It won't be long (until the next train trip!)

The Beatles might have been the main backdrop musically to the final years of steam, but there were other performers woven into that tapestry. I was always keen on pop music, and at school, I was often being asked what I thought of the latest releases, and who I was tipping for the top spot. I bought my first single in February 1964 for six shillings - 'Not fade away' by the Rolling Stones. At that time, a cop usually cost me less than two old pence, and so that record represented about 40 cops! I wished that steam wasn't fading away, but unfortunately it was, and so I was off to the Manchester area the same week with my two friends, Ian and Mike. It was my first trip with Mike, but it was far from the last, for most of the future trips that I made in the company of someone, that someone was Mike. Incidentally, as I have already mentioned, most of my train spotting friends tended to be older than me. Ian was about three years older, that is fifteen, and Mike, at seventeen, was really old, and he had a job! We'd visited Oldham Lees, which was on the point of closure, dashed round Bury, before tackling Bolton, which was a much weightier proposition, for it held 36 engines. All was standard L.M.S. fare, mostly 'Black Fives', 4Fs, and a number of 'Crab' 2-6-0s. There was still quite a few WD 2-8-0s allocated to the Midland Region in 1964, but they were to disappear at the end of the following year. Later in the day we travelled on to Wigan and Sutton Oak sheds. Like The Dave Clark Five, I felt 'Glad all over' at seeing so many new locomotives. At the time, it was too easy to take for granted the run of the mill engine numbers, for in places like the North West, there were so many steam engines still at work, that no one could have predicted that just over four years on, they'd all be gone.

In those early months of 1964, I managed an away trip about every fortnight. The above trip was fairly typical, in that the sheds targeted were in the North Western area of the London Midland region. This area was relatively easy to get to from Hull, largely thanks to the 'Trans-Pennine' DMU service to Liverpool. The Beatles might have been singing about love on their B-side hit 'You can't do that', but money, the timetable, and ultimately, my mam, said the same thing about travelling further afield in a day.

18

I compensated for this frustrating situation by visiting my local shed, Dairycoates, every day. Brian and I had a den there, right in the middle of the shed yard, yet out of the gaze of any predatory foremen. There were two dead end sidings, used for the ash wagons, which sloped down below the level of the surrounding tracks, and our den was behind one of the buffer stops at the end. From here, we had a grand vista of the depot, and periodically, like meerkats, our heads would pop up to survey all around us! At that time, Drapers hadn't started to scrap steam locos, and so the focus of our attention was definitely on the active visitors to this vast shed. As we were on the depot so often, one of the regular drivers got to know us, and so we got the opportunity to ride in the cabs of WD 90009 and B1 61306. However, the highlight had to be the offer to drive WD 90677 one day. It was only from the coaling stage to the disposal pits, but what a thrill it was for me as a twelve year old. I remember that the regulator was fairly easy to shift, and that there seemed to be a slight delay between this action and the subsequent movement of the loco. Then the engine just seemed to ghost along with a whisper of steam. Suitably excited, when I got home I placed the letter D, for driven, against the number in my abc Combined Volume! Other codes were R, for ridden on, and H, for hauled by. I was never a big fan of cabbing locomotives, like some, and so my abc Combined Volume has no C entries! Draper's were to be very late in the day entering the locomotive breaking business, but soon made up for lost ground once they got cracking! Until the sad lines of condemned engines appeared, Dairycoates was dominated by local B1 4-6-0s, WD 2-8-0s and LMS 'Coffee Pot' 2-6-0s. Elsewhere, I've seen the Ivatt 4MT 2-6-0s called 'Flying Pigs', but in Hull, they were usually called 'Coffee Pots'. Hull's remaining V3 2-6-2 tanks, which had been regulars on the Brough workers' trains, had just been transferred to Newcastle. The resident B16 4-6-0s, with their irregular 3 cylinder beat, were wheezing out their last few months on local freights, before they became the first engines to be devoured by Draper's torches at the end of 1964.

However, there were highlights. A1 4-6-2 60156 appeared on shed, out of steam, on January 31st, and stayed for a few days. Sister engine 60145 was sighted on March 25th, but by that time, A1s were not common around Hull, although 60147 was spotted as late as November 8th. When I found 43138 and 43141 stabled at the outdoor turntable on February 2nd, I was over the moon. My spotting book had them down as allocated to West Auckland, and prior to that, Scotland, but local spotters quickly realised that they had been transferred, and were to stay at Hull for a couple of years. O4 and 01 2-8-0s from Sheffield and Nottingham area sheds were almost daily visitors, but they became scarcer as 1964 moved into 1965. Until they were all withdrawn at the end of 1963, 02s had been regular performers. Indeed, on my first day at Riley High School in September 1963, I copped 63931 on Hull's 'straight line' from Dairycoates to Cottingham. I was fortunate, but the teachers probably unfortunate, in that many of the classrooms faced the Hull & Barnsley overhead route around the city, which at that time was very busy. The straight line was about 200 yards off to the west, behind some allotments, but at break times or during field games, I would keep a watchful eye in that direction. I must have been a confident lad, for within weeks of starting the school, I managed to sell the headmaster, who took us for maths, raffle tickets to fund the preservation of J15 65462!

Trainspotting was never far from my thoughts, and if I wasn't spotting at school, or at Dairycoates, I'd try anywhere locally. One jaunt took Brian and I to Spring Bank level crossing. There used to be a long carriage shed just east of there, which was demolished soon afterwards, and we dived into its depths, hoping to find some long withdrawn loco. All we found were coaches. However, like all great explorers, we were undeterred, and continued through Spring Bank cemetery, out the back, and over the Hull and Barnsley line and into uncharted territory. As we descended the railway embankment on the other side, our eyes fell on a very overgrown area of sidings. The site looked massive to a youngster's eyes, as there were probably ten long sidings, all covered with a variety of vegetation and even trees. We thought that we'd discovered some unknown branch, but looking back, the disused tracks were the defunct remains of the sidings near to the Imperial Standard factory, and reputed to have been used for the wool trade in the Second World War. A popular haunt where Brian and I spent many happy hours, particularly in the school holidays, was the playing fields at the south side of the Metal Box factory, which were nick-named 'Foggy Fields' for some reason. There was still a farm in the area, and an occupation crossing led to a field where we regularly made dens, and awaited the 'big game', that is, cops! Located next to the 'north branch', and opposite Dairycoates depot, you could get a view of the main line as it climbed the embankment, with goods traffic from the docks passing behind the overbridge next to Dairycoates West signalbox. Furthermore, all east bound traffic from Inward Yard went under the same overbridge.

A regular to watch for was the 6.50 pm fish train from Outward yard, which I usually saw at Hessle. It was normally a V2, often a York loco, but occasionally from further afield. Bank holidays were another delight, for excursions to Bridlington and Scarborough often brought unusual, that is, not local, engines to Hull. West Riding B1, 'Black Five' and Jubilee 4-6-0s were the main fare, with occasional stragglers from the Manchester area. At that time, most of my local spotting was undertaken with my close friend, Brian, who was the same age as me, and had also gone to Constable Street School. His Dad worked at the Dairycoates coaling stage, which we nicknamed 'The Coaly', but others called 'the Cracker'. You'd have thought that that would have given us some sort of entry, but it didn't. One evening after school we went down as usual to bash the shed, but were thrown out by the foreman. There was a footbridge over the running lines to St. Andrew's Dock, and there was a store for winter salt under the shed end of it. Brian and I decided to vanish into the store until the offending official had departed. However, as kids do, we started to lark about, throwing great chunks of rock salt at each other. The next thing we knew, a booming voice yelled at us to come out of the gloom of this cellar. When asked what we were doing, I replied 'mining'. We didn't wait around for the foreman's response to that gem of wisdom!

I had two trips in March, the first being to Warrington, Chester, Birkenhead and Northwich. What stands out now in my mind was the sheer number of engines seen on those days out. Warrington Dallam had five Jubilees on, along with a number of 4Fs. Every shed seemed to have at least one obligatory 'Jinty' 0-6-0T, but Birkenhead also held Fowler dock tank 47160, which was the only one I ever saw. Strangely, Birkenhead only had nine 9F 2-10-0s on that day, which was very different from the picture three years later, when the place had become '9F City'! Mold Junction seemed a long way out from Chester, but it held four ex GWR engines, Castle 4079 and Grange 4-6-0s 6846, 6850 and 6854. Obviously it was a change over place for Western Region locomotives, and yet you'd have thought that Halls would have been more common. The second trip was an excursion to Crewe, courtesy of Hull Tigers playing Crewe Alexandra. These excursions were a cheap way to get to some interesting locations, for money was always tight, but they invariably only gave about four hours at the destination. This was fine for the football fans, but lethal for us spotters. It meant that I had to run everywhere, so it was a case of 'the more you dash, the more you bash'! This was my first visit to this great place, but amazingly I did not see any Coronations that day, for I was to visit Stoke and Stafford sheds with my two friends, Ian and Mike. The privilege of copping my first Coronation was reserved for the following month. Stoke was a massive sprawling shed, and it held 48 engines that afternoon. Stafford was a much smaller affair, and only had 13 engines on, five of which were 'Jinties', and was to shut the following year.

On May 17th 1964, it was 'Here I go again' like The Hollies sang, for it brought another cheap outing in the shape of a trip to Derby with Mike and Ian. Strangely, this one was on a Sunday, and that created problems, for the service to Burton, Uttoxeter and later, Nottingham, was very poor. Burton still had an allocation of Jubilees, and four were on shed that day, 45557, 45618, 45620 and 45622. The other highlight was J94 68068. The rest were mostly 4F 0-6-0s and 8F 2-8-0s. Uttoxeter was a delightful little shed, with a solitary battery loco BEL2, hidden amongst eight steam locos, 42066, 42069, 42564, 42590, 42605, 42609, 45060 and the obligatory 'Jinty', 47587. We were to have attempted Colwick, but the Sunday service conspired against us and we only managed Nottingham, which held 49 steam engines. Royal Scot 46167, Jubilee 45684 and three B1s, 61087, 61161 and 61178 stood out amongst the rest. The failure to bash Colwick was to some extent compensated for by the journey past Spondon scrapyard. Fortunately, the DMU was travelling slowly at that point and I copped all seven locos on site, solitary O4 63754, and 'Coffee Pots' 43068, 43083, 43107, 43110, 43142 and 43152. Most had been withdrawn from Boston shed the previous December.

The Beatles were about to bring out their 'Long Tall Sally' EP in June. However, I was definitely not going to take the advice of one of the compilation's songs to 'Slow down', for I'd been given the task of organising a day tour of the West Riding sheds using a local rover ticket at the end of May. These were terrific value at ten shillings (fifty pence!), for they covered all the West Riding, including York, Skipton, Selby and Doncaster. I've always had a gift with planning and timetables, and so the local railway society knew that if anyone could pack the most sheds into a day, then I could. With much juggling, I managed to fit in seven sheds on our itinerary, all by train. We also squeezed in Doncaster at the end of the day, but more of that later. We started with Wakefield, 'WD City', for it held no less than 29 of the beasts, out of a total of 42 engines on shed! That was to be the case until it closed, very suddenly, in May 1967. Next was Ardsley with V2s 60843 and 60923. Also present were A1 pacifics 60133 and 60148. We then shot off to Bradford Manningham with just six locos on, and then to Low Moor with 18 engines on. Here there were 5 B1s and solitary Jubilee 45565. Travelling south we alighted at Mirfield, which held 17 locos, mostly 'Black Fives' and 8F 2-8-0s. We had our lunch on the bank opposite Mirfield shed and it was a delight to watch 3 WDs and 2 'Black Fives' pass on the four tracks laid out in front of us, as the sun shone down on our makeshift dining place. However, Normanton beckoned, with four 4F 0-6-0s and a number of WD 2-8-0s. Last, but not least, was Royston shed. Here, apart from five 4Fs, there were about twenty 2-8-0s on shed, either of WD or LMS origin.

Our journey back to Hull took us through Doncaster. When we arrived there, a glance at my watch told me that we had twenty-two minutes before our connection. The Ian Allan Engine Shed Directory gave the walking time as twenty minutes each way, never mind any time to bash the shed. Now, I'd been deprived of Doncaster shed on a previous visit in December, and so those twenty-two minutes seemed to offer a tantalising opportunity to right that situation. A quick vote was taken, and a number of the fastest, or the daftest, of us shot off down Station Road. It was worth it though, for this large Eastern Region shed held 54 steam locomotives. WD 2-8-0s dominated, but there was still a hint of East Coast super power in the form of four A1 Pacifics 60114, 60119, 60149 and 60157, and two V2 2-6-2s 60810 and 60887. The rest were B1s, K1s with five 9Fs. There was no sign of the depot's renowned and ferocious foreman. In fact, he would have had trouble catching us, for we all fairly rocketed down the lines of stabled engines. How we did it, I'll never know, but we arrived back with a minute to spare. The day came to a perfect end with the sun setting behind 'The Plant' and B1 61392, which was a cop for me, at the head of our train back to Hull. Dead on time at 10.47 pm, our train arrived back in Paragon station, and a party of twenty very tired, but very happy spotters, shambled away into the warm night. Not only was that day in May 1964 a classic case of the 'more you dash, the more you bash' principle, it was also the supreme example of the 'more cops for your coppers' tenet. The trip cost me thirteen shillings and five pence, that is sixty-seven pence in new money! For that, I'd copped 139 steam engines and had seen over 300. That worked out at just over one old penny per cop. In all my life, I've never enjoyed so much pleasure for so little outlay. The Beatles could well 'Ask me why' on their 'All my loving' EP, but back then, I knew exactly why I had to chase steam engines while they were still there to chase.

Chapter 4

A solo career

Until the summer of 1964, all my trips further than York had been made in the company of older friends, such as Ian and Mike. The Beatles' solo careers were years ahead, but mine was about to begin, even though I was still only twelve. On June 6th I stopped collecting diesel numbers, when I went on a trip over the Goole to Selby line on its last day. It was also the first day that I bought tickets for a line that was due to close, tickets which I have to this day. The following week I was due to go on another West Riding Rover ticket with one of the regular local spotters. However, he pulled out of the trip on the Wednesday. That was par for the course. I had a number of friends of my age, who swore blind that they would go with me on trips, but when it came to the crunch, they always let me down. Hence, all my early outings were with older, more committed (I think we all should have been!) spotters, and hence also my desire to 'go it alone'. Like Roy Orbison, I was going to say 'It's over', to my chaperoned spotting trips.

So it was, that with or without my mam's approval, I went on my first solo trip further afield. The day started out well, for MN 4—6-2 35012 on a special up north welcomed me at Leeds. In quick order I then did all the Leeds sheds, starting with Holbeck, which apart from Jubilees 45564 & 45568 was surprisingly empty. A dash over to Copley Hill produced A1s, 60117, 60128, 60130 and 60157. It was a long bus journey out to Neville Hill, but I was rewarded with three more A1s, 60131, 60134 and 60154, and no less than six Q6s. Also on shed were preserved N7 69621, and K4 3442 'The Great Marquess'. It was the first and last time that I managed these two Leeds sheds in steam days. Stourton was next, and finally, Farnley, which was another long journey. It always seemed a windswept place and only held eleven locos, with Jubilee 45562 taking pride of place. As usual, time was at a premium, and I'd lost time on the bus trips. I caught a train out to Skipton and took less than twenty minutes to bash the shed and be on my way back to Leeds. The shed held 17 engines, of which no less than nine were ex M.R. 4Fs. I was then off to York depot, which was always a delight. Sixty-four locos were on shed, including four A1s, 60121, 60126, 60150, and for the second time in the day,

60134. There were 13 B1s on shed, and no less than fifteen V2 2-6-2s. What a great shed to bash! Last, but not least on the day, was Doncaster. No sign of the fearsome foreman, and 59 engines later, I walked back to the station, having seen 26 WDs and four A1s 60119, 60128, 60139 and 60158. So it was that even in the summer of 1964, you could still see 14 different A1s in Yorkshire in one day. Happy times!

Now to my mind, the West Riding wasn't really that much further than York, so I needed something a bit more substantial to establish my solo career. The North East, that's the place I thought, and so on August 1st I was off to Geordie Land! 'A Hard Day's Night' LP dominated that summer, but new contenders for the pop crown were rising in the west. The Beach Boys released 'I get around' and there couldn't have been a more appropriate anthem for the day. As a serious trainspotter, I usually spent all my time on the move with my head out of the window in the carriage vestibule. This would have been a blessing to fellow passengers, for I sang The Beach Boys' song continually all day! 'Any time at all' was a track off The Beatles album, and the sentiment certainly applied to York shed, for I did the shed every time I was in the city. On that scorching summer day there were 75 locos on shed. What a tally, five A1s, 60126, 60138, 60141, 60143 and 60150, three A3s 60062, 60092 and 60112, and twelve V2s, so there was still plenty of ex L.N.E.R. super power to see. Also present were B16s 61421, 61434, 61448, 61454 and 61457, but they were withdrawn soon afterwards.

It was then off to Darlington, and the start of uncharted territory. My Combined Volume around the Q6 and J27 numbers was decidedly barren, but that was all to change that eventful day. Darlington shed, as I will always remember it, was home to an army of J94 tanks, and so it was that morning, with nine on shed. There were also four J72s there, 69003, 69011, 69019 and 69020. Darlington held the standby locos for East Coast failures, and two A3s shared the honours that day, 60036 and 60045. I notched up my first Q6s of the day with 63383, 63415 and 63439. It was then a dash back to the station and off to West Hartlepool, where the Q6 count shot through the roof, for there were no less than fourteen of them on the depot! Also present was V2 60901, and four J94s, 68019, 68023, 68032 and 68036. To cap it all, A1 60155 roared past the shed on an express. So far, the J27 count was poor, for apart from the two York regulars, 65844 and 65894, there were none at Darlington, and only 65841 at Hartlepool. That was to change though, for after passing a number of vintage N.E.R. engines hauling freights on the run up the County Durham coast, where, incidentally, I saw my first North Sea oil rig, I arrived at Sunderland. The walk to the shed was like a step back in time. The depot itself seemed from a different era, which in some ways it was. There were 11 J27s and 6 Q6s on shed, along with B1s 61022, 61035 and 61322, K1s 62026 and 62042 and solitary WD 90459. Things were looking up! As I set off for Tyne Dock from Sunderland station, A1 60134 pulled in on a summer relief.

Now if Sunderland was from a different era, Tyne Dock seemed to pre-date even that! The shed was huge, but very derelict. Any one who did not actually know this shed in the sixties would struggle to comprehend that it really was like stepping back into the Depression years. I was welcomed there by long withdrawn J72 68704, sitting in solitary splendour in the first roundhouse I came to. Sister engine 69025 was also on shed, but pride of place went to the 8 9Fs allocated there for the Consett iron ore trains, and no less than 12 Q6s. I passed little traffic on the way to Newcastle, but I was steeling myself for a tough nut, Gateshead. Friends had told me it was a tricky shed to bash, and so all my cunning would be needed. The sun was still streaming down as I rushed up the brick stairs and into this top link depot. I fair raced around, for time was very tight, and a moving target is harder to catch! There were three A3s, 60040, 60062 and 60083 on shed, along with four A1s, 60129, 60146, 60150 and 60155. However, I was disappointed that none of the depot's A4s were there, but at least there were 11 V2s present. Tanks were represented by V3 2-6-2s 67620, 67628, 67643, 67651 and 67690, for Gateshead was the last shed to have an allocation of them, and they were to be withdrawn that autumn. The old order was present in the guise of J72s 69005, 69023, with 69028 passing the shed.

It was then a ride out to the Northumberland coast on the Tyneside electrics. Blyth South shed held solitary K1 62022, and 12 J27s. and took only five minutes to do. I then shambled down to the river, for the Locoshed directory mentioned a ferry. Nothing could prepare me for the sight of the timber coal staithes that dominated the view across the water. I think it cost me tuppence to cross, and a short walk under this mammoth structure brought me to the location of North Blyth shed. Basking in the late afternoon summer sun after their day's duties were over, were 11 J27s and 9 Q6s. I did not see a soul as I wandered around gathering numbers, and I drifted back to the river without anyone knowing that I'd been there at all. I arrived back at Newcastle at 7 pm, and in the fifty minutes before my southbound express, I saw 61216, 60080, 67636 and 67678. I sang my head off all the way back to York, and arrived back in Hull at 10.45 pm. I'd copped 156 steam engines, and all for the cost of twenty-two shillings and seven pence. I now definitely had my solo wings! I think many who were born too late to experience those halcyon days find it hard to imagine how good those times really felt. Maybe we do remember them with rose coloured glasses, but I believe that given half the chance, most spotters would go back there tomorrow without hesitation. Yes, the past was a different country, the likes we shall never see again, but as The Beatles said, it was still fab to be there.

Bob Dylan sang 'The times they are changing', and so they were. Engines were being withdrawn every day, sheds shut practically every week, and the pop world was rocked when those boys from Newcastle, The Animals, released a single that lasted more than three minutes! 'The House of the Rising Sun' was the culprit, and it was to become another of my vestibule anthems. Having gained my wings, I wanted to capitalise on my new found freedom as soon as possible. Therefore, I set off for the Lancashire coast on August 22nd at 6.50 am. I really pushed the boat out on this trip, because I didn't get back to Paragon station until 12.16 am Sunday morning! My mother was really very tolerant. At Leeds City station I nipped quickly over to Central, now long gone, and caught a train to Todmorden, which passed Low Moor shed. Another quick change there and by 9.23 am, I was at Rose Grove. There were sixteen on shed, with three obligatory 'Jinties', 47333, 47344 and 47383. Surprisingly, there were only two 8Fs there. Unexpected guests were B1s 61034 and 61353. Moving further into Lancashire, I visited Lower Darwen, the shed on the hill. I still remember the long cinder path rising to the depot, even though it was the only time that I managed to bash the shed, for it had just shut when I next dropped in during April 1966. There were 19 locos on shed, mostly WDs, 'Crabs' and Standard 4 2-6-0s. However, they all looked wonderful to me, for nearly all were cops. Lostock Hall was somewhat more substantial, for the shed was home to 46 engines. Strangely, the most common type was WDs, not 'Black Fives', for there were no fewer than 12 on shed. Two ex M.R. 'Jinties' where on shed, 47201 and 47211, along with three of the larger class. Highlights were Jubilee 45703 and Britannia 70003, and to me, for rarity value, 0F 0-4-0Ts 47002 and 47008. A short run brought me into Preston, where surprise motive power for the run to Blackpool was B1 61034, which reappeared on Blackpool Central shed as I was bashing it. There were 21 locos on shed, with 'Black Fives' predictably being the most common. I was pleased to see Jubilees 45592, 45633 and 45681, but even more pleased to see Patriot 45512. The final shed of the day was Fleetwood. My memory may be playing tricks, but I believe I caught a tram out to this fishing town. All was quiet as I skulked around the shed, which held 25 steam engines. Most were 8Fs and 'Black Fives', but there were two 'Crabs', a WD, a 4F, and two obligatory 'Jinties'.

It was now time for home. Preston was alive with steam power, including another Patriot, 45527, and Britannia 70006. Incidentally, nearly all the trains that day were steam hauled, such was the railway scene in the North West, even in the late summer of 1964. It was a long haul back to Hull, especially as it was getting dark before I left the borders of Lancashire. On the way back, I marked the cops into my abc spotting book. There were 133 of them, and all for the grand total of 17/11! This was to be the last trip were the average cost per cop was under two old pence, for I now had nearly 2900 engines underlined in my book, so cops were now getting harder to come by. However, the sun had shone all day, and as I walked home from Paragon station after midnight on that humid night, I thought 'I'll be back'. This song from The Beatles 'Hard Day's Night' album summed it all up.

Chapter 5

You really got me!

Train spotting was a way of life for me, and I would use any opportunity to collect more numbers. Fortunately for me, Riley High School's History Department used to run trips to various locations of interest. They always hired a train, and on Tuesday July 21st 1964, one such excursion was run to Lincoln and Skegness. Lincoln shed had shut to steam in January, but I still saw over thirty steam engines that day, mostly around Doncaster, and managed to cop six of them. The tour of Lincoln Cathedral was of less interest to me than 8F 48378 passing through the station. The highlight of the trip was the two locos that I saw upon arrival at the seaside town. B1 61390, and 'Black Five' 44666, were slumbering in the sidings, waiting to take their trains back home. I used my time well in the town, for knowing that the direct line to Lincoln was to close, I purchased some tickets for my collection, which I still have. Furthermore, on that pleasant July evening with the sun gradually descending in the west, it was a pure delight to watch the two locos pull out of the East Coast resort. 44666 took the 7.07pm to Belper, and 61390 followed it at 7.26 pm, with the train to Derby (Friargate). I never returned to the town again in steam days, and so it is an image etched clearly onto my memory from over forty years ago. I copped B1 61003 'Gazelle' at Gainsborough on the way home, and the final treat of the day was the sight of J50 No.11 (formerly 68914), which I also copped, along with class mates Nos 12 and 14 outside Doncaster Works. All that fun, and in school's time too!

In the summer of 1964, V2s were still the mainstay of the evening fish trains, with 60886 being noted on Dairycoates on July 30th. 'Black Five' 4-6-0s were fairly regular visitors to Hull, often on excursions to Bridlington and Scarborough, and that was how I copped 45437 on Saturday August 8th. They tended to be less common on shed, but you did see them occasionally. I even visited Bridlington shed twice that year, more out of curiosity than hopes of a great haul of engine numbers! To my surprise, steam engines that arrived on excursions were still being serviced there, even though the depot had lost its allocation in December 1958. On Sunday May 31st, the shed was home to 'Black Five' 45034 and

B1 61173, but a visit on Friday August 21st only revealed B1 61158 in solitary residence.

The charts of August 1964 may have been dominated by The Beatles with 'A Hard Day's Night', and The Beach Boys with 'I get around', but a new musical force was to arrive in September. That force was The Kinks, and the opening riff of 'You really got me' exploded onto the scene in that month and it has never really gone away since. September was to be the month for two very special trips, each unique in their own way. At the time, all my train spotting trips had been out and back in one day, with the slight proviso that I occasionally rolled home after midnight, especially on the Wembley escapade of May 9th. That was all to change on the evening of Friday September 4th, for I left Hull on the 9.27 pm train to Doncaster, destination London, and then on to the South Coast. Along with my two mates, Ian and Mike, we were to travel overnight to Kings Cross, arriving there at the ungodly hour of 3 am, and we'd then walk the three miles across the Capital to Waterloo station. We only saw two steam engines on the way down, B1 61306, which hauled us to Doncaster, and WD 2-8-0 90130. The next sight of steam was Standard 2-6-4 tank 80154, which I copped, and Merchant Navy 4-6-2 35014, which I didn't cop, at Waterloo station. The time was just after 4 am, and we were due to travel on the first express out to Eastleigh. Nearly everything I saw was a cop that day, for my only previous incursion onto Southern Region metals had been on my first trip to London in the May. It goes without saying that the day, which was brilliantly sunny, was a visual feast of Southern steam super power. Not that lesser classes were not appreciated, for Q1 0-6-0 33004 was a pleasure to see on leaving London.

It was only a short walk from Eastleigh station to the depot, and that beautiful September morning revealed no less than eighty steam locomotives on shed. There were twelve West Country pacifics, and seven of the Battle of Britain class. However, to my consternation, there were no Merchant Navy engines evident, but that was rectified during the day, for I saw eight of the class in total. Engines worthy of note on this vast depot were five M7 0-4-4 tanks, all in for scrap at the neighbouring works, which I never managed to visit, even on subsequent trips to the area. They were 30029, 30052, 30108, 30129 and 30667. They'd had a long and useful life, but 1964 was to be the last summer for these old timers.

Four more Q1s were noted, along with two Q 0-6-0s, 30546 and 30548. Highlight of the visit, in a diminutive sort of way, went to the two A1X 0-6-0 tanks awaiting preservation, 32646 and 32650. I'd not seen any members of this wonderful class before, so that was an unexpected treat. At the time, the Southern Region did not tend to take long to dispose of redundant locomotives, so any withdrawn engines copped were a bonus. There were exceptions, for some K 2-6-0s hung around on the South Coast for a year after mass withdrawal. Furthermore, there was some reluctance on the part of shedmasters to let the final members of the well loved Schools 4-4-0s go, and bid them farewell on their last inevitable journey to the breaker's yard.

Our next stop was Bournemouth. Having never travelled that far south in my short life, I couldn't help but notice how warm, indeed tropical, it felt on that late summer's day. It was positively balmy, and as I've noted earlier, it did seem that the sun shone a lot more in those far off days. Maybe it is just imagination, or the trick that your mind plays as it filters the memories selectively through the intervening years. Whatever it is, I enjoyed a lot of very sunny train spotting trips throughout 1964. So it was that before lunch, under a burning sun, my mates and I found ourselves trudging around the gravel and clinker that comprised Bournemouth shed. It was a busy depot, but only had sixteen locos on display, with Standard 5 4-6-0 73112 'Morgan le Fay' passing the shed as we quickly scribbled numbers down. There were three West Country pacifics on, 34034, 34045 and 34105, and just one Merchant Navy pacific, 35011. The rest of the engines were mostly Standard classes, with three Ivatt 2-6-2 tanks to add a touch of variety.

We left the town for a destination that was very different, the Isle of Wight! Steam power was the order of the day on all expresses. However, it was the last few days for steam power on the West Country trains, for they were dieselised en mass the following week, resulting in the withdrawal or transfer of all the pacifics from Exmouth Junction shed. Not that we knew that as we journeyed to Portsmouth. A short ferry trip brought us to Ryde Pier Head, were O2 0-4-4 tank number 14 'Fishbourne' hauled us to St. John's Road Station. The shed had six more class mates basking in the late summer sun, 22, 26, 28, 29, 33 and 35. We saw more on our short island hop, and my tally of O2s had reached thirteen by the time we boarded the Portsmouth ferry once more.

We had spent less than two hours on the island, but it left a lasting impression on me. I was fortunate enough to visit it one more time, in December 1966, to travel on some of the last steam services just before electrification.

Our next shed was something of a surprise to me. Guildford on the way back, or Nine Elms as we passed through London once more would seem to be in order. That was not to be, for the leader of our band of three, Mike, had chosen Fratton. This shed in Portsmouth had lost its allocation of engines as long ago as November 1959, but still saw active service with the many visiting locomotives from around the region. Therefore, Standard 4 2-6-0s 76011, 76012, 76061 and 76067 were to be expected, along with Standard 4 2-6-4 tank 80010. However, what I did not know, as a twelve year old roaming innocently around in a world that didn't possess the instant communications that we now take for granted, was that the shed held the preserved locomotives of the Southern Region. So it was that a stroll through the roundhouse entrance revealed the splendour of M7 0-4-4T 30245, T9 4-4-0 120, 0298 2-4-0WT 30587, N15 4-6-0 30777, Lord Nelson 4-6-0 30850, Z 0-8-0T 30952, and two Schools class 4-4-0s 30925 and 30926. What a perfect end to our Southern shed bash, for the journey back to 'The Smoke' only produced ten more steam engine numbers, with USA 0-6-0 tank 30064 being a neat cop for me. We left Kings Cross about 6.30 pm, and only saw three more steam engines on our long journey home, for it was dark soon after Peterborough. We arrived back in Hull Paragon at 10.22 pm, having been away 25 hours, but I'd copped 152 numbers, mostly Southern, for the grand total cost of 47/9! I had had practically no sleep, but like The Beatles had sung on the 'Hard Day's Night' LP, I'd do that 'When I get home'! So the summer holidays of 1964 came to an end on a high note.

The next trip couldn't have been more different, for it was relatively local, to the East Midland sheds, and it was the first time I travelled by minibus to depots. Mike had arranged the trip, and because we were motorised, the aim was to bash as many sheds as possible. So it was that on September 19th we left Hull at 6.30 am, bound for our first port of call, Hasland, near Chesterfield. This proved to be a disappointment, for it had shut two weeks previously, and only had six locos on, mostly 4F 0-6-0s. Perhaps reflecting the mood, this trip was conducted largely under overcast skies. It was only a short hop across to Westhouses, which had fourteen engines on shed. Four more passed on freights during our brief visit, but the pattern for the day was already emerging, lots of ex Midland 0-6-0s and L.M.S 8F 2-8-0s, that was until we hit the Eastern Region sheds. Travelling by road had the advantage of speed, but of course, you didn't cop anything en route. There was one further snag, and that struck next. On our way to Kirby-in-Ashfield the minibus broke down! All our plans crashed to the floor as we paced around the local garage, waiting for the mechanic to sort out the clutch. What seemed hours passed as they repaired the offending part, but in reality, it was probably only one hour. However, it cost us a depot or two that day. What should be playing on the garage radio, but 'You really got me'! Kirkby-in-Ashfield continued the order of the day, with Johnson 0-6-0T 41712 thrown in for a bit of variety. Also on shed was 9F 92008, and a brace of WDs, 90408 and 90448.

Annesley, although very close to Kirkby, was a total departure engine wise. We'd seen hardly any of the ubiquitous 'Black Fives' so far, but this shed held six of them. More importantly, there were three Royal Scots, 46112, 46122 and 46163 dumped at the back of the depot. Jubilee 45735 and eight 8Fs made up the rest of the L.M.S contingent. O4 2-8-0 63661, and B1 61185 were the token Eastern Region locos, but nineteen of the forty one engines on shed were 9F 2-10-0s, including Crosti-boilered 92025. Now I've said that when travelling by road you don't see engines en route, but that wasn't strictly true that day, for unbeknown to all the party, our travels took us past Bulwell Common. Lo and behold, a line of locomotives hove into view as we passed the scrapyard there. The yard held Patriot 4-6-0 45535, and five O2 2—8-0s, 63925, 63939, 63956, 63980 and 63985. So we arrived at Nottingham depot, which held few surprises, apart from B1 61042, Jubilee 45564 and Britannia 4-6-2 70051, with thirty locos in total on shed. The depot was running down steam rapidly at the time, as was our next location, Toton. There were thirty four steam engines on shed, but there were diesels everywhere, mostly 'Rats', that is Sulzer type 2s. The presence of ten WDs was unexpected, and only the sight of Jubilee 45684 broke the pattern established on the Midland sheds visited that day.

The last two visits of the day were firmly in Eastern Region territory, although Colwick, our next destination, was to be transferred to the Midland Region at the end of 1965. This impressive shed had fifty seven engines present, mostly O4 2-8-0s and WDs. It also had ten L.M.S. 2-6-0 'Coffee Pots' on shed, but the highlight for me was the stationary boiler, K3 2-6-0 61943, which even then had been withdrawn two years. Nine apiece of the B1 and 9F classes made up the final total. Under sunny skies we then arrived at our final destination for the day, Langwith. No less than twenty two O4 2-8-0s were on shed, along with a solitary O1, 63650. The total of thirty seven steam engines on shed was completed by a tally of fourteen WD 2-8-0s. I arrived back in Hull at 9.40 pm, the trip having cost me 26/9. Herman's Hermits were right when they sang 'I'm into something good', for I'd copped 179 locos, and that worked out at just over two old pence per cop. But I wasn't finished for that weekend, for I was to do a shed bash the following day. You might think, like The Beatles said, 'You can't do that', but you'd be wrong, for Sunday saw me doing Frodingham and Goole sheds.

Chapter 6

I feel fine

On Sunday September 20th, my dad left behind taxi-ing, and returned to the sea. He was due to report to the wharf at Flixborough, to take up the position of Chief Officer on the coaster 'The Kirtondyke'. I used the opportunity to travel with him by car, and persuaded him to visit Scunthorpe 'on the way'. He still owned the 1958 Vauxhall Victor, registration YRH 114, that had helped him earn a living through the severe winter of 1962/63. The car was to belong to him until 1975. Leaving my dad in the car, I rushed around Frodingham depot. By 1964, most steam locomotives were dirty, but Frodingham depot positively excelled at the art of grime. Namely, you could tell a Frodingham loco by its pure filth, but you couldn't tell its number! That Sunday, the shed held fifty four engines, of which 35 were WD 2-8-0s. All required close scrutiny to ascertain their numbers. You dreaded passing a 36C loco on a trip, for that was Frodingham's shed code, as your chances of accurately identifying the number were slim indeed. There were fourteen O4 2-8-0s on, and the remaining locos were B1s 61110 and 61157, 9Fs 92198 and 92199 and solitary K1 number 62035. My dad must have been in a good mood, for I then persuaded him to wait at Goole, while I walked the cinder path from Mariner Street to the shed. There were ten WDs on shed and a brace of L.M.S. 2-6-0 'Coffee Pots' 43098 and 43125. I managed to cop twenty one numbers that sunny Sabbath, and at absolutely no cost to yours truly! This was fortunate, for the recent overnight trip to the Southern Region had severely depleted my funds. Therefore, it was to be over a month to my next serious shed bash.

As I couldn't keep away from railways, in the interim I did two things, one usual, one unusual. The usual involved going around Dairycoates shed at least once a day. By late 1964, there were no local locos to cop, and visitors from further afield were now thinning out. Also, I'd seen many of the ones that regularly visited Hull from Staveley, Doncaster, and other sheds in that area. As a change from train spotting, I decided to visit the Hornsea and Withernsea branches. They were due to close at the end of October, so I took the opportunity one Saturday to travel both lines. Local L.M.S. 2-6-0 'Coffee Pot' 43079 was the only steam engine I saw all day, for it was working the yard at Hornsea Bridge, and took the local freight out at 11.00 am, bound for Hull. Wisely, I bought as many tickets at points on the lines as I could afford, but the purchases were definitely counted in pennies, not shillings! Again, I remember this autumn day as being very sunny, almost unseasonably so.

Musically, the autumn was dominated by the release of The Beatles first film, not surprisingly called 'A Hard Day's Night'. They revisited Hull for the third time on October 16th, and once more appeared at the ABC Theatre. Not that I went to see them, for all my money was committed to following steam, and anyway, at the time I was more of a Rolling Stones fan! In those days there was a bit of rivalry between the fans of these two supergroups. Meanwhile, away from Planet Pop, and on Planet Shed Bash, travelling by road seemed to have become the norm, for my next trip, down to Peterborough, and visiting the East Coast mainline sheds on the way back, was also by road, but in a more uncomfortable mode. This time, I was to be dead weight in the back of an A35 van. In other words, I'd been asked along to share petrol costs, but I didn't get the benefit of the one passenger seat! The van belonged to Tony, a chap from the local youth club, and Mike, surprise, surprise, had the passenger seat! So it was that on Saturday October 24th, an ageing green van was hurtling down the Great North Road, to rendezvous at Stoke Summit, south of Grantham. We left Hull at 6 am, to get the best spot to view A4 pacific 60009 'Union of South Africa' hauling a northbound special. Once more, the day was sunny, with the Gresley loco flying past under a gorgeous autumn sky. Into the bargain, WD 90195 and 9F 92180 rumbled past on freights. It was still early as we parked at New England shed, 34E. The first sight that met us was a very grimy and derelict 9F 92176, which was obviously due for scrapping. Twenty two engines were on shed, with 9Fs being the most predominant class, closely followed by 'Coffee Pot' 2-6-0s. The highlight to me was the two A3 4-6-2s 60062 'Minoru' and 60106 'Flying Fox'. They were to be the last A3s to be in steam in England, with the last three members of the class ultimately eking out their final days north of the Border. At the back of the shed was another surprise. Just like Colwick, New England had a resident stationary boiler, and once again, it was a K3 2-6-0, number 61912. The shed was due to close to steam in January 1965, and the K3 was to be the last locomotive dragged away, finally being scrapped two and half years after it had been initially withdrawn.

Our tiny van then bounced its way back to Retford, where the two sheds were still kept busy with the East Midlands coal traffic. It was all to alter radically the following June, when a new railway bypass allowed Tinsley shed to take over the rosters and eliminate steam working in the area. Nevertheless, the former Great Northern shed had four B1s, two K1s, O4 2-8-0 63692 and two WD 2-8-0s on. The former Great Central shed was somewhat busier, with twelve locos on shed. There were four WDs, and the same number of O4s, with fellow engine 63688 passing the yard as an added bonus. The O2 2-8-0s, once a staple of the Retford area had long gone. Indeed the last time I'd seen one was in Bulwell scrapyard in September. No trip to the area was complete without a visit to Doncaster, and so in the early afternoon, we rolled up outside the shed. No problems from the resident foremen this time, so we whizzed around the site, recording fifty engines on shed. There were still four A1 pacifics present, 60114, 60139, 60149 and 60157, but they were to disappear from the Eastern scene within weeks. Doncaster was using B1 4-6-0 61060 as a stationary boiler, and four other members were on shed, with classmate 61061 passing the depot as we went round, closely followed by O4 63818. There were no less than nineteen WDs on shed, with a further four O4s keeping them company, along with ten 9Fs.

It was then on to the last shed of the day, one of my favourites, York. I'm sure that some people must have had trouble doing the shed, but I never did. Once again, we sailed around without a single challenge. For our efforts, we were rewarded with a tally of fifty locomotives. Even at this late date, A1 pacifics tied jointly with K1 2-6-0s as the most plentiful class on shed, there being ten of each. York still had its two resident N.E.R. old timers in the form of J27s 65844 and 65894. The L.M.S was represented by six 'Coffee Pot' moguls, two 8F 2-8-0s, consecutively numbered 48621 and 48622, and pride of place, Jubilee 45642 'Boscawen'. It was then home to a well earned bath, needed to smooth out the aches and pains of a twelve hour day in the back of a van. It wasn't as though I'd had exclusive use of the goods area, for one other poor soul also had bounced his way around the country with me, but time has erased his name from my memory! For my pains, I'd only copped twenty seven numbers, but my pocket was 16/2 the lighter!

During October 1964, an event took place in Hull that was to have widespread implications on the railway scene, not just locally, but nationally. The last of the B16s had been withdrawn, and by this date, their normal ultimate destination, Darlington, had stopped dismantling locomotives. It therefore fell to local scrap merchant, Albert Draper, to buy the Hull B16s and break them up at his Sculcoates yard. 61420 was the first to go, and local enthusiasts 'bulled up' the loco at its final resting place. That is, they gave it a final polish so that it would look its best for the breakers. The other B16s followed during November, but no one thought too much of the event. Little did I know that the scrap dealer had developed a taste for redundant steam locomotives that would see over seven hundred more engines follow these chosen few into his yard within the next five years.

My mother was definitely not keen on me travelling in the winter months, so it was with some difficulty that I managed to sneak in a trip to Worcester on November 14th. She was concerned for my health but like the Fab Four, I told her 'I feel fine'! Hull City were to play Kidderminster, and so a football special had been arranged for that date. The excursions had the benefit of extreme cheapness, but the disadvantage, to serious train spotters like me, of a very late start, that is 8.30 am! Once again, I travelled with Mike, and we had planned to do Kidderminster shed, but a recent issue of 'The Railway Magazine' had noted that the depot closed to steam during August. No instant communications in those days! Now one of the advantages of departing late on a November morning was that it was light all the way to our destination. This meant that we had a very fruitful journey down through the Midlands. We passed many O4 and WD 2-8-0s, handfuls of L.M.S. 8Fs and 'Black Fives' and not a few 'Coffee Pot' 2-6-0s. However, there were some real gems on display that autumn day. Starting with Doncaster, we saw preserved A3 pacific 60103 'Flying Scotsman', and passing Derby we somehow gained a view of the engines preserved there; 2-4-0 158A, 4-4-2T 'Thundersley' and 4-2-2 118. My log book notes over ninety steam engines on the way down, and the ultimate pride of place fell to G2 49407, which was hauling a final special before withdrawal. I was to see the last remaining G2s a few weeks later at Bescot shed, but this was the only occasion that I saw one in steam, somewhere near

Walsall, I believe. Once onto former Great Western territory, we saw a variety of ex G.W.R. motive power. It was always a pleasure to see their distinctive locos, for they operated far from home. Of all the regions, my tally of Western numbers was always the poor relation among the others.

At Kidderminster we raced out of the station to catch a bus to Worcester, while all the football fans trudged off to the ground. Obviously we would have caught a train had there been one, but our arrival fell between convenient times, so this line of attack was adopted. However, not only was the journey fourteen miles, and so took nearly an hour on bus to get there, but we had quite a lengthy wait for it. This meant we had to be quick, for the excursion home left about half past five, and it was already after three when we got to Worcester! There were over thirty locos on Worcester shed, all ex G.W.R except for two 'Black Fives' 44777 and 44919. Two of my favourite Western engines, Castles, were present in the form of locos 5000 and 7005. Three Halls 5979, 5983 and 6934, four modified Halls 6995, 7906, 7920 and 7928 and three Granges 6861, 6877 and 6878 were also on shed. The works was adjacent to the shed and so we wasted no time, quickly mopping up the seven locomotives within its bounds. They were 2291, 4619, 6169, 8104, Castle 7011, Grange 6856 and last, but not least, 8F 48309, which, being allocated to Somerset and Dorset territory at Bath (Green Park) was a real triumph for my abc spotters book. There was a convenient train back to Kidderminster, and so we rushed back to rejoin our fellow Hull bound travellers and board the special back home. It was dark by then, but we still managed to grab a few numbers through steamy windows as our diesel multiple unit rattled its way homeward. The trip cost a mere 18/4, and I managed to cop 85 new numbers for my book. The sun had shone, but it wasn't the warmest of days. My mother remonstrated that it was to be the last train trip until spring, but with approximately forty steam engines being withdrawn every week, I had no intention of being out of the spotting scene for that long. But there again, as The Beatles sang on the B side of 'I feel fine', 'She's a woman', so how could she possibly understand!

Chapter 7

Eight days a week

Because my travels were curtailed by my mam in the winter of 1964, I spent a great deal of time going around Dairycoates shed. Finding A1 60147 on shed on Sunday November 8th was a triumph for me, for in spite of many trips on the East Coast main line that year, this A1 had eluded me. However, the real surprises arrived in December. It seems strange to me after all these years, that despite my regular and frequent visits to the shed, it fell to my friend Ian to break the glad tidings on Sunday December 13th, that 7 section held some Gresley pacifics for scrap! Surely, it was cruel joke, in time for Christmas. I'd had tricks played on me before, because at that time, I loved running, and I would run the mile to the depot. I was an easy target for anyone who wanted to start rumours like 'there's a streak on shed!' A streak was the local nick-name for a Gresley A4 pacific, and was sure to send any serious spotter running. However, Ian was a good mate, and so I set off running in the shed direction. It was dark, and there was a light covering of snow, but there was no mistaking the impressive outlines on the sidings reserved for stored carriages and locomotives. From the distant lights of the shed yard, I could make out the grimy silhouettes of A3s 60071 'Tranquil', 60085 Manna', 60091 'Captain Cuttle, 60092 'Fairway', not one, but four Gresley pacifics! I copped 60085, and after thanking Ian for the tip, he informed me that A3 60080 'Dick Turpin' was at Draper's yard at Sculcoates. So it was off to the yard to take my chances. Incidentally, 60091 was the first A3 I ever saw, when it visited Dairycoates in 1962. How were the mighty fallen! That Sunday was the very beginning of a long and sad procession of steam locomotives from other parts of the country that were to be dismantled at Draper's yard, first at Sculcoates, then later at Neptune Street.

So 1965 arrived, and it was to be the best of years, and also the worst of years. I'd just turned thirteen in December 1964, and I don't know if 13 is unlucky, but the year proved to be very different to the previous one. It started out well, for just as January 1964 had brought an L.M.S named 4-6-0 to Hull on an excursion from Liverpool, namely Patriot 45531 'Sir Frederick Harrison', January

1st 1965 saw Royal Scots 46122 'Royal Ulster Rifleman' and 46156 'The South Wales Borderer' arrive in Hull for scrap. I've already mentioned that it always seemed to be sunny in my train spotting days, well, 1965 ultimately proved to be the wettest summer since 1910! There were some sunny trips, but even now I seem to remember it being overcast on most days out.

The Beatles had released another top selling album on November 27th 1964, 'Beatles for sale'. One track hit me straight a way, 'Eight days a week'. It could have been written for me, because that's how many days a week that I wanted to go trainspotting! I don't know how I managed it, but somehow I persuaded my mam to let me go on a trip to Birmingham on January 2nd, right in the middle of winter. I must have told her, like The Moody Blues, that I had to 'Go now! I left Hull on the 6.13 am to Doncaster, a regular turn for me. I saw over fifty steam locos on the way down, which wasn't bad, as it was dark until I got to Sheffield. It was a bitterly cold day, with ice and snow across the land. I arrived in Birmingham New Street at 10.21, and after stumbling through the chaos that was the station rebuild, in an attempt to find the ticket office, I managed to board a local train to my first shed, Saltley. There were over thirty engines on shed. Pride of place went to Jubilee 45674, but the biggest surprise was Hull WD, number 90704! I was to see several Hull engines at Saltley over the next two years. A short hop by local train brought me to Aston, which held sixteen engines, including Britannia pacific 70018 'Flying Dutchman'. It was now lunch time, and I distinctly remember eating my cucumber sandwiches on the station as I waited for the train to Bescot. It was extremely cold, but the sun was shining, I swear! Bescot was busier, with nearly forty locos within its yards. Crossing the footbridge from the station, I was confronted by the classic outlines of the four remaining L.N.W.R 0-8-0s, 48895, 49361, 49407 and 49430, standing in snowy surroundings on the scrap roads. Two G.W.R engines, 0-6-2T 6671 and Modified Hall 7908 raised an eyebrow, but otherwise, all was pretty standard stuff, 'Black Fives' and 8Fs. However, the shed was graced by the presence of Britannia 70052 'Firth of Tay'. Another short journey brought me to Wolverhampton, where what seemed an interminably long bus trip brought me to Oxley shed. What pure G.W.R. heaven! Nearly all the fifty six locos on shed originated from the Great Western, including my favourites, the Castles, which were represented by 5026, 5056, 7011, 7012, 7021 and 7023. A few 'Black Fives' and

8Fs had intruded, but the whole shed oozed the atmosphere of the G.W.R. The depot also oozed copious amounts of dirty smoke from the slumbering engines, but what a smell, and what a great atmosphere it was! The final destination was the small shed at Bushbury, which like Aston, I only bashed this one day. It only held fourteen locomotives, with 9F 92057 being the most interesting (and massive). It was then a mad dash back to New Street, for my train left at 6.18pm, and it was already pitch black when I left Wolverhampton. Incidentally, in 1964, British Railways went over to the continental 24 hour clock, and so from now on, times like this will appear as 18.18. I got home at 11 pm, and my mam immediately sent me up for a bath, not only to get the filth off me which I always collected, but also to warm me up! I thought it was worth it though, for it was an area that I hadn't explored before, and so I copped 132 engines for a cost of 23/8. That worked out at just over two old pence per cop, but it was to be almost the last time that I bought cops so cheaply.

A long procession of withdrawn locomotives passed through Dairycoates on their way to Drapers yard, and it would be tedious to list them all, but my diary does highlight A3s 60036 'Colombo' and 60045 'Lemberg' on February 13th. Nearly all classes of engines that existed within a hundred miles were being brought into the city to satisfy Draper's insatiable appetite for scrap. It was in February that I made the first mistake of the year, for I got a friend interested in trainspotting. What's wrong with that, you might ask? Well I soon found out. To break him in, so to speak, I arranged a local trip to Immingham, a shed I'd never visited. Therefore, on Sunday February 21st, we took a trip on the paddle steamer across the Humber, and caught a train to Habrough. From there we walked the three miles to the depot. On the way we were taunted by some local lads, who thought that our Riley High School scarves marked us out as boys from a rival school. However our scarves were ultimately to save the day. Immingham shed is in the midst of dock property, and I thought, erroneously as it turned out, that the shed would be easier to do on a Sunday. We'd finished the shed, which held thirteen B1s, fourteen WDs, eight 9Fs and an O1 and O4 apiece, when we heard a cry to stop right were we where. That was our call to scarper, but where to? Our train didn't leave Habrough for another three hours, for the Sunday service was appalling. The transport policeman must have realised this somehow, and we were soon apprehended. His opening line floored us 'Are you from Riley High School?' It was useless to deny it, for our scarves gave the game away. When we admitted that we were, he wrote out a note, and asked us to forward it to his old maths teacher at the school, who I remember was nick-named 'Tiny Tim'. He was about 6' 6" tall, and built to match, but for the life of me, I can't recall his correct name. He was a real gentleman, and rarely had trouble with the kids. At the time, he was deputy head master, and I believe he would have made an excellent head, for as you will read further on, the current headmaster did not do me any favours. Anyway, for our troubles, the transport policeman gave us a lift back to Ulceby station, and thanked us for passing the letter on! All's well that ends well, but we now had three hours to wait for our train. Like many stations then, Ulceby had gas lighting, and the lamps were glimmering brightly as the New Holland train finally rumbled into view after dusk.

The following Saturday, I'd planned to go with Trevor, for that was the novice spotter's name, to Liverpool. He stayed at our house Friday night, in order that we'd both be ready for the 05.36 departure to Leeds the following morning. It was always stressful organising myself for the eventful days that I planned, but taking Trevor was a bridge too far. We managed to get to Edge Hill shed, but by then I was running a colossal fever, and Trevor's enthusiasm for the ways of the shed basher was rapidly diminishing. I noted over thirty engines, including Jubilee 45563, before it was full tilt for home. The Coronations that I had hoped to mop up had obviously already gone for scrap, and that trip was to cost me very dearly health-wise, for I was off school for five weeks. I didn't even get out of bed to visit Dairycoates for nearly three weeks, but when I did, five K1 2-6-0s 62020, 62033, 62040, 62066 and 62070 had joined the ranks on death row. My illness was very infectious, so I was not allowed to attend school. However, there was no problem with me getting some fresh air, which I invariably did by visiting the shed! I also started to collect ships about this time, and later in the year, that decision was to prove very beneficial to my trainspotting.

My mother no doubt bent my ear about travelling around in the winter months, but spring was just around the corner. Once I'd regained my strength, I planned my first trip of the season, solo, of course! It was to be to the Midlands on Saturday March 27th, which turned out to be a sunny day. I started out on one of my regular turns, the 06.13 to Doncaster, where I zoomed around the shed. There were forty locos on shed, but the A1 pacifics and V2 2-6-2s had gone, leaving just legions of WDs and a few B1s and O4s. My next destination was Canklow, which was at Rotherham. It was a fair bus trip out to the shed, and the depot held thirty locos, mostly WDs and a number of 'Black Fives' and B1s. After travelling via Sheffield Midland, and passing Jubilee 45593 'Kholapur' on the way, I alighted at Chesterfield Midland, where I was to sample the delights of the two Staveley sheds. This necessitated a four mile bus ride into the unknown, and the wait for the bus was so long that it cost one shed visit that day, Derby. As the area was very unfamiliar to me, I asked a local where the engine shed was. His reply shook me 'Are you looking for a job?' Travelling half fare, it would never have crossed my mind that I could be mistaken for a fifteen or sixteen year old. I said that I wasn't, and I got the directions anyway. Staveley (Great Central) held fifteen locomotives, mostly 2-8-0s of the O1, O4 and WD classes. Many of them had visited Hull in previous years, and so it was not a very fruitful visit. However, Staveley Midland was a different kettle of fish altogether, for the shed yards were home to over thirty engines. Most were 'Coffee Pot' moguls and WD 2-8-0s, but in residence were Johnson 0-6-0T 41835 and two Deeley 0-4-0 tanks, numbers 41528 and 41533. I took the opportunity to nip into the local works, and saw four more Johnson tanks at work, 41708, 41734, 41763 and 41804.

Time was getting on, and even though I knew that Derby was off the agenda that day, I hurried on to my next port of call, Nottingham. The journey took me right past Derby shed, where I managed to grab eleven numbers, mostly 8Fs and 'Black Fives'. Spondon dump was still scrapping locos, and I noted 2-6-4Ts 42165, 42284 and 42291 on the site. Whilst passing Trent Junction, a flash of brilliant green and shining brass metalwork announced the passage of Castle 7029 'Clun Castle' on a special to the north. When I arrived at Nottingham, what a sad spectacle the Midland shed made, for there were just seven steam engines on shed, 47231, 47645, 48046, 48156, 48405, 78062 and 92068. The depot was to close to steam the following week. It was then time to head homeward, and feeling elated, I reverted to my old practice of vestibule entertainment, that is, I sang 'Eight days a week' at the top of my voice all the way back to Sheffield. It was no wonder that I got colds, for all my journeys were conducted with the vestibule window open, and my head stuck out of it most of the time! With the light finally failing at Mexborough, I noted the last number of the day, WD 2-8-0 90202. I arrived back in Hull at 21.22. The trip had cost me 14/10 and I had only copped 46 locos, but it felt great to be back in the saddle once more, free, and on my own. If you had asked at the time what was great about being a trainspotter, I'd have replied, like The Beatles 'Every little thing'.

Chapter 8

Ticket to ride

I managed four trainspotting trips in April 1965, which matched my May 1964 record total of monthly outings. The Beatles released a single on the 9th that was tailor made for rail enthusiasts, 'Ticket to ride'! April 3rd found me hanging on for dear life as a pillion rider on a Honda 50. My friend Mike wanted to visit North Lincolnshire, and so it was, at a top speed of thirty miles per hour, we trundled out of Hull and headed for Stainforth. Even though the Eastern Region was to be completely dieselised within twelve months, the Doncaster, Scunthorpe and Immingham lines still saw a considerable amount of steam operation. We observed fourteen steam engines on a variety of freights, with WDs predominating. A solitary B1, number 61370 from Canklow, and two 9Fs also made an appearance. Fortunately, it was a sunny day for our al fresco journey, and in brilliant sunshine we headed off to Scunthorpe. Frodingham shed held over thirty engines, mostly local WDs, but L.M.S. 8F 48037 was an interloper. There were still a number of O4 2-8-0s around, with the usual livery of pure grime, but this class was declining rapidly at our next port of call, Immingham. No transport policeman this time, and we came away with a haul of thirty numbers, mostly WDs, 9Fs and B1s, with only two O4s, 63650 and 63868 in the yard. Then it was back to Hull, via the New Holland ferry. Only nine cops that day, but it didn't cost much.

As I've mentioned, the History Department of Riley High School ran excursions, and the next one, on Wednesday April 7th was a gem, to Darlington shed and Hexham! The tour guide was to be Mr Goode, who'd been a master at the school, and a leader of the former school railway club. Our special ran as 1Z02, and it was a special day, for even passing York shed yard, I copped a Tweedmouth A1 60152 'Holyrood'. I'd already bashed Darlington shed twice before, and so I was not expecting too much in the cop department. However, I managed five cops, as Darlington works had started to take over steam repairs from works that no longer undertook them. That explained the presence of four L.M.S 8F 2-8-0s on the shed. The most populous class were the WDs, but the depot still held nine of its popular J94 tanks, that seemed to busy themselves on local trips. The last hint of L.N.E.R. express power was there in the form of two A1 pacifics, 60124 'Kenilworth' and 60155 'Borderer', and a brace of V2 2-6-2s 60806 and 60884. The special then got under way to Hexham, for a visit to the Abbey. To my delight, our return journey took the excursion past Gateshead shed. I've seen a number of dates for the dieselisation of the depot, but I can vouch that there were no steam engines on the shed that day. However, I did strain my eyes at the repair shed at the western end, for I seemed to make out the distinct profile of a steamer in there, but all to no avail. So we headed south and home. I may have only copped ten locos that day, but it was a day off school, and all expenses were paid by mam, to boot!

By this time, Albert Draper was on overdrive scrapping steam engines. April 1965 brought many ex Midland 4F 0-6-0s to Hull, along with Jubilees 45565 'Victoria' and 45592 'Indore'. Pride of place that month went to A1s 60126 'Sir Vincent Raven' and 60140 'Balmoral', two of the ten broken up in the city. The influx of foreign motive power, albeit for scrap, all helped to fill spaces in my abc Combined Volume, but there was a tinge of sadness as I underlined the diminishing ranks of steam numbers in my book. However, there was more than a tinge of sadness on Sunday 11th. In the last chapter, I commented that 1965 was the best of years, and it was the worst of years. The worst was about to happen. I'd had friends prosecuted for trespassing, the most recent case while they were spotting in the Newcastle area, using a redundant signalbox as their viewpoint. However, I thought that I was too quick to get caught, but I was to be proved wrong that Sunday. My friend Brian and I went down to Dairycoates spotting. At that time, many older coaches, often L.N.E.R., were being broken up, and we'd rummage through them looking for tickets to collect. I found a real gem that day, a single from Glasgow (Queen Street) to Mallaig. Even the name conjured up visions of exotic travel and exciting new locomotives. The coaches were in an appalling state, for many had been vandalised, with glass everywhere. Unbeknown to us, we were being watched by British Transport Police, who nabbed us and hauled us off home. With head bowed, I apologised to my mam and to the officers, and hoped it wouldn't go further. My mam banned me from the shed, which I sort of kept to, well, for a week or two anyhow!

However, it didn't stop me from doing a relatively short hop the following Saturday, April 17th, to the Nottingham area. This trip is a mystery to me, for I have clear recollections of the many, many, shed bashing trips I took, but this one, after forty years, is a total blank. That may say something about my memory, but luckily, I do have the notebook to confirm that it really took place! In those days, I regularly visited the information office at Paragon Station, on the look out for pamphlets on bargain fares. Some were very glossy brochures, but many seemed to use very nasty paper, A5 size, and be printed practically illegibly in orange or pale red ink! I left Hull at the unbelievably late time of 11.55, and because the journey took us on some closed lines in the Shirebrook area, I strongly suspect it could have been a football special to Mansfield. This was precisely the kind of excursion that would have been printed on one of the nasty leaflets mentioned above. I saw over twenty steam engines on the way, and from Mansfield I used local buses to transport me to the selected depots, the first of which was Langwith. The shed had changed considerably since the previous September when I'd visited it, for there had been a huge influx of freight super power, in the form of fifteen 9F 2-10-0s. There were still eleven O4s on and four WDs, but the old order was changing. It was then off to Kirkby-in-Ashfield shed, which was filled almost completely with L.M.S. 8Fs, twenty nine of them, with eight 4F 0-6-0s making up the final tally of thirty seven. The cost of only 12/1 suggests a cheap day excursion, but I still managed to cop thirty engines that day.

My mother's embargo can't have been too strict, for on the 24th I was off to that Mecca for all railway enthusiasts, Crewe. Into the bargain, I'd added Shrewsbury, with the promise of more G.W.R. locos, Stoke and Stockport to the itinerary. In fact, anywhere in the area that started with S was included, but by this date, Stafford shed was on its last legs, steam-wise. I was to leave Hull at 05.36, but I detect my mother's hand in the revised send off of 06.50, and the 21.17, not 22.46 arrival back into Paragon station! I was to travel via Leeds, Stalybridge, Stockport and Crewe, with the first shed bash being Shrewsbury. I saw nearly forty steam engines en route, and even at this late date, there were surprises. Leeds City station was home to A1 60131 'Osprey', whilst classmate 60154 'Bon Accord' was resting on Farnley Junction shed. I saw, and copped, Jubilee 45596 'Bahamas' at Stockport, for it had eluded me on my visit there in December 1963. My vestibule anthem that day was quite naturally, 'Ticket to ride'! Shrewsbury was a new location for me, and I shot off to the shed, for as I've mentioned, I tended to run everywhere, such was the energy of youth. Also, by trimming two and a half hours off my day, my mam had put great pressure on my schedule. However, I was not the sort of soul to be defeated by things like this. Too many steam locomotives to see, and so little time! The shed was a bit of a disappointment, for although it held thirty three engines, the Great Western was only represented by three pannier tanks, a 2-8-0 2895, 0-6-2T 5677, Hall 5933, and the class for which the town was famous for, Manors. Three of them were present, class members 7801, 7803 and 7812. But there was no time to waste, and so it was straight off back to Crewe. It seems strange now, for I then zoomed straight off to Stoke, but I suspect that the compressed scheduling was the real reason here. The Beatles were singing 'I'll follow the sun', but I wasn't that day, for it was distinctly overcast everywhere I went.

Stoke was a massive shed, and I'd bashed it once before, in March 1964. It was home to no less than seventy one locos. As I remember it, you had to be careful with the shed, as you could miss a bit off, if you rushed too quickly around the vast site. Obviously, the depot was crammed with ex L.M.S stock, but a number of Standard class 4 4-6-0s and 2-6-0s were starting to edge in. These types were to become more common in the closing months of steam operation at the depot. The shed always seem to harbour a nucleus of 'Jinties', in this case numbers 47273, 47280, 47596 and 47649. My note book suitably chock full of numbers, I returned to Crewe, and ran across the footbridge connecting the station to the adjacent shed. It was to be the last time that I did the shed, as it was to close the following month. Gone were the Coronation pacifics, and in their place was Standard motive power, in the shape of the Britannia class. No less than sixteen members of these 4-6-2s were present, with most of the rest of the contingent of thirty five locomotives being made up of 'Black Fives'. A solitary Jubilee 45563 'Australia' spoke of former glory days, but it was all over, bar the shouting, for this one time bastion of former L.M.S. super power. There was a nod in the direction of a former rival, the G.W.R., in the guise of Grange 4-6-0 6851 'Hurst Grange', but unfortunately, I did not cop this engine. Crewe South shed beckoned, and I was welcomed at the shed by 6851 again! It had obviously trundled down while I'd walked down Gresty Lane. The sprawling shed yard held sixty two engines, with four classes predominating, 'Black Fives', 8Fs, 'Coffee Pot' moguls and 'Jinties'. There were two apiece of 4F 0-6-0s, numbers 44373 and 44593, and Britannia 4-6-2s, numbers 70039 'Sir Christopher Wren' and 70053 'Moray Firth'. It was about this time that the first Britannias, numbers 70007 'Coeur-de-Lion' and 70043 'Lord Kitchener', were withdrawn.

I was then off to Stockport, my final port of call that day. Usually, I would have done Heaton Mersey depot as well, but once again, the truncated time-tabling was taking its toll. Edgeley shed was not that far from the station, and a ten minute yomp found me within the bowels of the smoky building. There were twenty five engines quietly simmering away at 9B. This shed code was to become better known three years on, when it became one of the last steam depots to survive, closing in May 1968. Midland 4Fs were fading from the scene, as only 44394 was present, but it was a pleasure to record three Jubilees, numbers 45596 'Bahamas', 45654 'Hood', and for the second time that day, 45632 'Tonga' lurking in the shed. Like many before, and not a few after me, as I left I stood at the top of the steep cinder path that was a landmark of this location, and took one long last glimpse at the shed. Smoke was rising lazily from the shed vents, and the air was redolent of partly combusted coal. With this memory in mind, and the acid tang of soot in my mouth, I walked thoughtfully back to Stockport station and the train home. If someone had asked me at that moment if this was what trainspotting was all about, I would have replied, as The Beatles did on the flip side of 'Ticket to ride', 'Yes it is'!

Chapter 9

Help!

My next jaunt was on May 1st, and like the year, it was to be the best of days, and also the worst of days. In the seven days since the previous trip, I must have sweet talked my mother, for the departure time was back once more to the 05.36 Leeds train. Liverpool was to be my target on that day, for I had been robbed of its treasures in February, when ill health had deprived me of valuable cops. At least it was light at this time, and so I noted over thirty engines on the way. A class cop for me at Leeds City was Clan 4-6-2 72008 'Clan Macleod', one of the few remaining members, based at Carlisle Kingmoor. All was typical L.M.S. fare, even down to 'Jinty' 47357, fussily shunting Liverpool Lime Street Station as I arrived at 10.05. I then travelled under the Mersey to make my second visit to Birkenhead depot. This shed was always a hive of activity, becoming 9F City in its final years. There were ten members present that day, along with four 'Crabs', nine 8Fs, five 'Jinties' and eight L.M.S. 2-6-4 tanks. Amazingly, there was only one 'Black Five' on shed. It was then back under the river, and a short bus ride brought me to Edge Hill. This maze like shed held over thirty locos, and having made sure that I did the coaling road on the other side of the bridge, my final tally included two Britannias, numbers 70017 and 70052. I was delighted to see two Jubilees still extant at the shed, 45590 and 45633, but only the first was a cop for me. As usual, there was no time to waste, for Speke Junction beckoned. To me this shed always seemed to inhabit a nether world somewhere between total desolation and civilisation, for it covered a vast cinder strewn area. That day only twenty four locos were present, with 'Black Fives' being, by a slight margin, the most common. That was all to change before steam finished, because Speke became home to many 9Fs, most dumped awaiting disposal.

My itinerary then took me up to Bank Hall. I'd been forewarned about his location, for it could be a difficult nut to crack. The entrance to the depot was via a passage that descended some steps that ran straight past the foreman's office. Armed with this knowledge, I became two foot tall, only regaining my normal height when my feet touched the trackside. Bank Hall was a small shed, containing just fourteen locos. The depot was one of the last on the Midland Region to be allocated Jubilees, and on that hot and sunny day, it held four examples, 45627, 45684, 45698 and 45721. It was then time to become two foot tall again, ascend some steps, and head for Aintree. Things looked up here, for there were nearly forty engines present, with L.M.S. 8Fs predominating. Six WDs graced the yard, the largest contingent that I had seen on a Midland shed for a while, but all members of the class were to vanish off the region within months. As Aintree was home to many race meetings, the shed played host to a variety of visitors, and this day was to be no exception, in the form of B1 61024 'Addax' from 56A, Wakefield shed.

The afternoon was nearly over by the time that I set foot at Wigan, with Springs Branch shed firmly in my sights. I'd been to Wigan in February 1964, but Mike, the leader of our gang, had wanted to do Wigan depot before it shut. Therefore, this was my first chance to notch up this classic depot on my score card. It was a fair walk from the station, but it was worth it, for within its hallowed walls there were sixty five steamers on shed. Engines of note were Jubilee 45563 'Australia' and Stanier 2-6-0s 42948, 42953, 42960, 42961, 42963 and 42968. The depot was to be a bastion for this small class in steam's final years. Aintree's tally of six WDs was surpassed by the presence of no fewer than eight of the class at Springs Branch. I must have gained time on the trip, for the hastily scribbled 9K on my note book front denotes that I managed to fit in Bolton at the end of day. The local train out of Wigan was hauled by Fairburn 2-6-4T 42249. As we chugged past Ince, an amazing vista came into view. I gasped, as my coach, high on an embankment, rattled slowly past a vast scrapyard that was laid out below me, like some trainspotter's wildest dream. The low evening sun cast shadows among the sea of steam locomotives that stretched out as far as the eye could see. My pen, in readiness, quivered at the prospect, but like many an old Klondiker searching for gold, I was to be disappointed, for only 'Jinty' 47584 remains scribbled on that page to this day. I could see the boiler tops of a Coronation and a number of 'Jinties' and L.M.S. 2-6-4 tanks, but the engines were so closely packed together, that all but one of their ranks eluded me. To add insult to injury, I didn't even cop the 'Jinty'! Trainspotter's heaven had turned in slow motion to trainspotter's hell! As I've said, it was the best of days, and it was the worst of days. I estimated that there were about eighty engines on the site, and all attempts to acquire their numbers failed. I even wrote to the yard, but they never replied. However, the day could get worse, as I was to find out.

Bolton was not the problem though, for this shed, like Springs Branch, was another first for me. It had been my intention to bash the shed in December 1963, but my friend Ian had baulked at the prospect of a dash in the dark on that winter evening. Oh for the bliss of travelling solo! The shed was sizeable, holding forty seven locos. 2-6-4 tanks, 8Fs, Ivatt 2-6-0s and the inevitable 'Black Fives' comprised the majority of the allocation. Only one Midland 0-6-0, number 44311 was present, but still hanging on was Johnson 0-6-0T 47202. The obligatory 'Jinty' was represented by 47520. It was then off to Manchester Exchange, and a long journey home that gave me plenty of time to reflect on what might have been. However, I had copped 133 steamers that day for 24/4, which wasn't bad at all by that date, and it was to be the last time that cops came so cheaply. I walked into the house after 23.00, to be greeted by my mam, holding a letter asking me to attend juvenile court on charges of not only trespassing, but also vandalising railway property. Things could get worse, and they had! Like the Beatles that summer, I needed 'Help'!

This was worse than I thought, for I hadn't been vandalising coaches, but who would believe me. Secondly, this could spell the end of my shed bashing days, and I was only thirteen! Like The Rolling Stones, I could hear my mam saying this was to be 'The last time'! The court appearance came and went. I was fined one pound, and warned of the dangers of trespassing on the railway. However, I believe that the conviction led to my 'demotion' from 2A that school year, to 3B the following school year. In the exams that summer, I only averaged 52.5%, which was hardly surprising, having missed half the spring term due to illness. However, a friend did even worse, with 52.4%, and he stayed in the A stream. I suspect that the headmaster took an unfavourable stance on miscreants! My mother must have really put the dampers on my activities this time, for the next trip was five weeks away, on June 5th, and was only to York. Even then, I had to go with another friend from school, Ralph. I was under strict instructions not to trespass on the shed, but of course I ignored it! The shed was home to thirty eight locos, including three A1s, 60121 'Silurian', 60152 'Holyrood' and 60156 'Great Central'. By this date, York was quite a focal point for the remaining V2s, and nine were on shed that day. Ralph and I spent the rest of the day spotting from the south end of the station. Even at this late stage, we saw over sixty steam locomotive movements between 09.00 and 18.00. However, only five were on passenger services, the most notable being V2 60837 heading north from York in the morning.

Something must have happened during the following week, for out of nowhere, an overnight trip to the Southern appeared for Saturday June 12th. My mate, Mike, must have convinced my mam that I'd be O.K. with him. It was already light when we arrived at Waterloo station at 04.15, and we were hauled by 34051 'Winston Churchill' a loco famous that year for hauling the great man's funeral train. Our destination was Guildford, for a trip on the Horsham branch on its last day of operation. Ivatt 2-6-2 tanks 41287 and 41299 were to be our motive power on the line. As usual, I bought a few tickets as souvenirs of the memorable day. In the light of recent events, I then did something very rash. Guildford shed was a semi-roundhouse depot that faced the station platforms. The temptation was too much for me, for I had never done the depot before, and so I made a lunge for the shed yard. I didn't get far though, for I tripped and nose-dived into the ballast, with my face not ten inches away from the third rail! I wonder how Mike would have explained my early demise to my mother on his return. I didn't get to do the shed that day, but I wrote to the shed foreman the following week, and he very kindly listed the engines on shed for me, so all's well that ends well. There were only two U 2-6-0s on shed that day, numbers 31619 and 31627, but the yard was full of N 2-6-0s, eleven in total. Two Q1s, 33018 and 33026, and Q 30535, all cops, were ultimately to be added to my tally. It was then off to Basingstoke, another strange location, where the depot had lost its allocation in March 1963, but remained open to service steam right up to the end in July 1967. The shed held ten locos, including three pacifics. L.M.S. 8F 48638 from Westhouses was a long way from home, but it wasn't a cop for me. Eastleigh beckoned, and the afternoon found us strolling around the depot, with sixty engines on. The twelve Southern pacifics were to be expected, but by this time, the loco works was taking in jobs from other regions, and so five 'Coffee Pot' moguls were there, along with 9F 92153, amazingly also from Westhouses, and fellow loco, 92206 from York. Two L.M.S 8Fs, 48217 and 48408 added to the multi-regional feel. It was then back to Waterloo and home. I even managed to cop a WD at Doncaster, 90285, a Retford regular, but not for long, for the shed closed the following Monday! The time for copping large amounts was now past, for I only copped 67 engines, for an exorbitant cost of 36/1! The day of the cheap cop had come to an end, but I still loved my spotting travels, and I could certainly sing along with The Hollies at number one, 'I'm alive'.

I must have been wheedling my way into my mother's good books, for in no time at all I was helping Mike plan a real biggy, a week in Scotland. A few weeks earlier, all had looked very black for me, and if anyone had asked how I felt, I would have had to reply, like The Beatles on a B side, 'I'm Down'! I got busy contacting B&Bs, and booking the railrover ticket. It was about this time that the 'straight line' from Dairycoates to Cottingham shut, and the new Cricket Circle curve at Anlaby Road was commissioned. I lived closer to Anlaby Road crossing than Dairycoates crossing, and so I got to see more of the excursions that passed through Hull to the coast. Not that they were crossings any more, for both flyovers were now in operation. I had started my train spotting days in the summer of 1962 at Dairycoates gates, and I remember them being very wide. They caused immense delays to road traffic, for the crossing was very busy, and so it was a great relief to all road users when they closed for good later that year. I can also picture the Engineer's depot, just to the north of the crossing and beside the 'straight line' mentioned above. In 1962 and 1963, J94 68042 was often to be seen shunting there, but in later years the resident Ruston & Hornsby 0-4-0 diesel shunter was the sole occupant of the yard. Anlaby Road crossing lasted a while longer than Dairycoates crossing, finally succumbing in August 1964. My favourite spot was on a raised piece of waste ground near the Cricket Circle. On one side was the Victoria Dock branch, and on the other side, not thirty yards away, was the curve to the Cottingham line. I could therefore look down on the local freights towards the east, or west toward the excursion traffic as it slowly negotiated the severe curve on its way to the seaside. Steam was still very common on these specials, with B1s, 'Black Fives' and Jubilees making many appearances that summer. I noted 45604 'Ceylon' on Saturday July 3rd, and 45675 'Hardy' the following day.

There was one more trip to be made before the epic Scottish shed bash, and that was on Thursday July 1st, courtesy of Riley High History Department. The destination was to be Chester, and you can judge how active steam was by the tally of seventy five locos seen en route. I had no chance to do the shed, but I still copped 32 numbers that day, all at no cost to myself. A highlight for me was Jubilee 45697 'Achilles' as our train passed Wakefield, for the ex Lancashire & Yorkshire route seemed to be the preferred one by B.R. for excursion traffic. We also passed Mirfield and Patricroft depots, and the cop of two Midland 0-6-0s, 44294 and 44522 at Warrington Bank Quay gave the trip an early boost. Amazingly, the final word came from my local shed, Dairycoates, for Jubilee 45664 'Nelson' of Leeds Holbeck was under the coaling stage, and it was a cop! The Beatles might sing that 'You've got to hide your love away', but I had absolutely no intention in the summer of 1965 of doing that.

Chapter 10

Satisfaction

The Beatles were riding high in the summer of 1965, with the release of the single 'Help', the film of the same name, and an eponymous album in August. However, the Rolling Stones were also huge, and like everyone else, I was seeking 'Satisfaction'. On Friday July 23rd, Mike called round and asked if I had got my currency sorted out for north of the border. Panic ensued as I turned to my mam in despair, and looked down at my Bank of England notes. However, it was just a wind-up on the part of Mike! The following day, July 24th, Mike and I left Hull. We could sing along with The Animals in the pop charts, 'We gotta get out of this place' as we boarded the train to York, via Market Weighton. The direct line was still open, and we headed along it towards my idea of satisfaction, Scotland. The 'North Briton' arrived late at York behind A1 60154 'Bon Accord', a Neville Hill engine. That late start cost us a visit to St Margarets shed that day. I noted no less than eighteen locos as we headed north past York depot. You soon learnt the ability to write rapidly, without looking down at the page. There were four A1s in the shed yard, and the cop of Jubilee 45608 'Gibraltar' got the day off to a good start. It was sunny as we left Yorkshire, but torrential rain was falling by the time we reached Edinburgh. A4 60010 'Dominion of Canada' on Darlington shed caused us to scratch our heads, but as we were soon to find out in the press, it was due into the works for restoration work, preparatory to going to Canada. I copped B1 61019 as we passed Heaton shed, and it was pleasing to be greeted into Scotland's capital city by York A1 60129 'Guy Mannering', appropriately named after one of Sir Walter Scott's novels. The whole holiday was to be very wet, and our view of the Waverley line was severely curtailed by the constant steaming up of the windows. Our first port of call north of the border was the tiny depot at Hawick, which held just two locos, 76049 and 78047. However, I was fortunate to see, and cop, A4 60027 'Merlin' as it passed through the station. It was then back to Edinburgh and Dalry Road shed, with twelve engines on, mostly 'Black Fives' and B1s. A bag of chips and a walk to the Y.M.C.A. brought the day to a close.

A feature of the holiday was my spending money. My mother had allowed me a sum, I believe it was about two shillings and sixpence a day, to feed myself. That is, twelve and a half pence in modern currency. This may seem positively miserly in the twenty first century, but I had every intention of making a profit on it in 1965! To achieve this, I lived on bags of chips at 6d, and my speciality, Gala apple pies, at 9d each. Of course, I also devoured all I could at breakfast at the B&B places we stayed. On Sunday morning, in pouring rain once again, we caught a bus to Clockmill Road and St Margarets depot. What delights it held! There were only thirty locos on shed, but what a variety, fourteen different classes were within its bounds, surrounded by the tenements that were a feature of this location. Stationary boiler J36 65234, A2 60530 'Sayajirao', A4 60027 again, and the last A3s in service, 60041 'Salmon Trout' and 60052 'Prince Palatine' were at home. Class mate 60100 'Spearmint' was nowhere to be seen, and it was only when we received the next issue of 'The Railway Magazine' that we found out that it had just been withdrawn. A delay of two months in getting information was normal then. The days of the internet, mobile phones and instant communication lay at least two decades away. Nearly everything I saw on my Scottish break was a cop, for I'd never been north of the border before, and only seen the odd Scottish loco at Carlisle or Darlington. After recording six V2s and A1 60129 preparing itself for the run south, we headed to Waverley station for the 10.00 departure to Glasgow Queen Street, which by this date was the only Glasgow station that didn't allow steam engines to grace its platforms.

Five Glasgow sheds fell in quick succession. Even though we had Scottish Railrover tickets, we used buses most of the day, for it was the Sabbath, and trains to the depots were thin on the ground, if not non-existent. Motherwell, 66B, held twenty locos, mostly 'Black Fives'. Incidentally, in Hull, they were nicknamed 'Mickeys', for a reason that escapes me now. 9F 92076 was an interloper from 12A, Carlisle Kingmoor. Next was 67A, Corkerhill, a depot in a surprisingly pleasant suburban environment. It held twenty eight engines, and a visitor, Jubilee 45660 'Rooke' from Leeds Holbeck, was a cop for me. Standard 4 4-6-0 75012 from 6A Chester, was a long way from home, but as we were to find out later in the week, Cowlairs was taking in steam work from all over England to keep busy. Like most of the shed visits that day, 'Black Fives', Standard 5 4-6-0s and 4 2-6-4 tanks were the accepted order. The next location could not have been more different, Polmadie. It was the only time on my many travels that I felt threatened, for the area was exceedingly rough, and youths eyed Mike and I suspiciously as we sloped into the shed. We had passes for all the visits that week, for that was one of the conditions that my mother had laid down for this extensive trip. The Scottish Region was always generous with their provision in regard to permits, and individual sheds rarely checked the details. Therefore, the day and the time of our visits didn't always coincide with the written letter of the law! 66A held thirty six locos, mostly of classes of the accepted order of the day. A2 60535 'Hornet's Beauty' was dumped at the back of the shed, with a yellow stripe across its cab side. This denoted that it was not to work south of Crewe, but its chances of doing that looked mighty slim, for it had been stored there for months. Jubilee 45697 'Achilles' from Leeds Holbeck was also present. It soon occurred to me on this holiday that English locos seemed a lot more common on Scottish sheds, than Scottish locos did on English sheds. I'm sure there must have been a reason for that, but I never found one.

Mike and I were glad to get away from Polmadie and on to St Rollox. The area was slightly better, and the depot held two A4s, numbers 60019 'Bittern' and 60034 'Lord Farringdon', out of a total of thirteen engines on shed. Our final call that day was Eastfield, which held twenty locos. The sight of six B1s and a solitary J38, 65910, my first cop of the class, was most welcome. It was then back to our digs. To give an idea of how tight I was keeping the purse strings on this holiday, I only bought a cup of tea for 6d, and a bag of crisps for 4d that day! It was all in a good cause though, because any money saved would fund my next trip.

Monday found us exploring the delights of the former Glasgow and South Western Railway, Ayr being our first visit. Exactly half the tally of twenty six engines on shed were 'Crabs'. It was Stranraer next, holding just eleven engines, with Britannia 70005 'John Milton' taking centre stage. We passed Troon scrapyard on the way to Kilmarnock, but we only managed to note down Clan 72005 'Clan Macgregor' and two Fairburn 2-6-4 tanks, 42148 and 42179. A long bus ride brought us to Hurlford, with its imposing architecture. Five 'Crabs', long time residents of the Ayrshire coast, mingled with 'Black Fives' and Standards there. It was only tea time, and so before we dossed down for the night, we headed for

Greenock. In torrential rain, we trudged around Ladyburn shed, which was home to five 2-6-4 tanks, three Standard 2-6-4Ts, and a solitary 2-6-0, 76071. I lashed out that Monday, for I bought not one, but two Gala pies, and a bag of chips!

Tuesday started sunny as we journeyed out to Stirling depot, which held eight 'Black Fives'. It was then into Fife, and Dunfermline. Firmly in L.N.E.R. territory, my score of J37s and J38s started to rise, along with rare Scottish WDs. The weather was still pleasant as we alighted at Thornton Junction. 62A seemed to be spread out and windy, but I copped nearly everything in sight. The depot held two J36s, 65327 and 65345, which was in use as a stationary boiler, along with seven J37s, and no less than ten J38s. With thirty one engines on shed it was like Scottish heaven to me. The Beatles could say 'It's only love', but it was real enough for me. The weather still held for our run to Dundee, where nestled in the shed were three A2s, numbers 60528 'Tudor Minstrel', 60530 'Sayjirao' and soon to be preserved 60532 'Blue Peter'. The old order was represented by J36 65319, and five J37s. Out of twenty five steamers present, there were also three V2s and eleven B1s. The weather continued to hold for our dash around Perth, which held nearly thirty locos, of which twenty two were 'Black Fives'. Pacific power was present in the form of A2 60512 'Steady Aim' and Britannias 70010 'Owen Glendower' and 70041 'Sir John Moore', both from 12A Carlisle Kingmoor. The final shed of the day was 65F, Grangemouth, which held over twenty locos. Three J37s, 64580, 64592 and 64610 represented the last of the old order. Also present were four WDs, four 'Black Fives' and a variety of Standard tender types. The sky was distinctly overcast as we headed back to Glasgow.

Our trip south on Wednesday was positively wet, wet, wet! We visited Parkhead 65C, for the five preserved engines stored there. I'm glad that we did, for in the ensuing downpour I got my one and only glimpse of Highland Railway 4-4-0 54398 'Ben Alder', for it did not survive to tell the tale, which was a great loss for the preservation movement. Carstairs held just twelve engines, including A2 60522 'Straight Deal', but at least that was more than the two banking engines at Beattock! We were then Carlisle bound, and in pouring rain we trudged around Kingmoor shed, home to over seventy locos, 39 of which were 'Black Fives'. I did this shed a number of times, but this was the only occasion that I got soaked doing it! All four of the last Clans were present, 72006 to 72009, along with six Britannias, four Jubilees and the last two Royal Scots, 46128 and 46160, which were on the scrap line. The real surprise that day was the presence of no fewer than four V2s, numbers 60816, 60824, 60846 and 60970, which suggests that this class was popular and well utilised to the last. 12B, Upperby, held nine Britannias, a number of Midland 4Fs, and the inevitable 'Black Fives'. It was then back to Glasgow via Dumfries. We never managed to do the shed that week, and the following year, when I did manage it, the shed had closed a few weeks before. Such is life!

We left our digs in Glasgow for the last time on Thursday morning, and made our way to Polmadie again. For some reason, now lost in the mists of time, we only did part of the shed, and then moved on to Cowlairs Works. Engines from all over the country lay within its walls, and I will list them in their entirety: 43023, 44758, 44769, 44874, 44882, 44886, 44949, 45404, 45478, 60031, 61349, 73000 and 73025 (from Shrewsbury!), 73125, 75020, 75024, 75026 and last but not least, 90560. A number of these locos were from the North West of England, and so were familiar to me. We then left Buchanan Street station for Dunfermline, to mop up a few stragglers, before heading decisively north to Aberdeen. As I've stated before, journeys were conducted on a head out of window, smoke in your eyes basis. Even so, we missed a southbound express near Stonehaven. I believe that A4 60004 'William Whitelaw' was the loco, and I never caught up with it, even though it was among the last A4s to be withdrawn. It was a pleasant evening as we sauntered around Ferryhill shed. Only twelve locos were on shed, but A4s 60006 'Sir Ralph Wedgwood', 60009 'Union of South Africa', 60019 'Bittern' and 60026 'Miles Beevor' were kept company by A3 60052 'Prince Palatine'. It was then chips and back to the B&B for Mike and I. Incidentally, our digs were close to Kittybrewster depot, but we didn't bash the shed, for it had shut to steam in 1961. However, I do seem to remember the sight of the coaling stage towering over the end of the street.

Friday was our last day in Scotland, and we intended to make the most of it. The sun was shining and it was the brightest day of the holiday. We retraced our steps to Ferryhill shed, were 60027 'Merlin' had joined its four fellow class mates, and V2 60844 'St. Peter's School York A.D. 627', a cop for me, was stabled nearby.

Dundee was again revisited, along with Thornton Junction, Dalry Road and St Margarets. I still managed to cop a few, even though I'd visited them recently. A new location was Bathgate, which was reached by a lengthy bus ride from Edinburgh. The shed was home to three J36s, 65267, 65282 and 65297. Also on shed were five Standard 4 2-6-0s and four Standard 2 2-6-0s. I copped everything there, except 76119. By evening there was no escaping the fact that our final call home was approaching, and we left Edinburgh about 23.00. I was all for bashing York shed in the wee hours, but Mike, who was due to head south on another holiday that very afternoon, was not keen. We arrived back in Hull at 05.03 on the morning of Saturday July 31st. My regret to this day is that at the time, I did not have the funds to follow him, for he was to visit all the remaining steam sheds in South Wales, Gloucester, Worcester, Bristol, Exmouth Junction, Westbury and that most special of lines, the Somerset & Dorset. That holiday would have filled many a gap in my abc, but it was not to be. It was always the Western Region that seemed to elude me, and as it was the first region to dieselise, time was not on my side.

At the end of the day, what had I come away with? I'd cleared most of the Scottish numbers I needed, I'd bashed all the remaining Scottish steam sheds, bar Dumfries, and I'd copped 467 engines. It had cost me a grand total of £10/19/9, but hey, what a gig! I had steam in the blood, and like The Beatles, that summer I could sing 'I need you'. However, I had to make the most of the relationship, for in three years, it would be dead.

Chapter 11

Yesterday

Plaintively, Paul McCartney sang 'Yesterday', and on Sunday August 1st 1965, I could have joined in with his melancholy song. I'd arrived back from Scotland the previous day, Mike was now somewhere in the South of England seeing engines that I was never destined to see, and I'd only memories of my recent holiday for company. A trip to Scunthorpe with my dad would normally have lifted my spirits, but I didn't cop any of the thirty locos on Frodingham shed. Everything seemed flat, boring, and anything but fab. What I needed was a plan, and I soon had one, in the form of a trip to the North East. In the meantime, my aunt had bought me a bike, and Brian and I biked to Goole on Sunday August 8th. I had considered it as a possible means of transport to sheds, but after arriving back in Hull with a very sore backside, I decided that this plan was a non-starter! Not that it was out for other guys. I remember a small coterie of dedicated cyclists who did just that. Their main man was Gordon, and like a few others, whose names escape me, he thought nothing of cycling to the South Yorkshire and East Midlands sheds and back in a day. That was a round trip of probably one hundred and fifty miles! Not surprisingly, these bikers had a certain confidence, if not arrogance about them. I can picture them now on street corners near the Boulevard, or outside the Youth Club on Gordon Street, bronzed, cocky, assured, sitting astride their expensive racing bikes. However, at that time, long distance cycling was definitely out for me. Unbeknown to my mam, I was back up to my old trick of visiting Dairycoates depot whenever I could. Jubilee 45661 'Vernon' and 4Fs 43865, 43991, 44386 and 44528 graced 7 section the following week.

August 14th saw me heading north on the 06.55 to York. I had thirty minutes in the town, and I used it to bash the shed. A1 60151 'Midlothian', a cop for me, passed the shed as I entered. Over fifty locos were present, with no less than six A1s still hanging in there, along with nine V2s, four J27s and visitor Britannia 70031 'Byron' from Carlisle Upperby. I passed A1 60145 'Saint Mungo', destined to be the last survivor of the class, at Northallerton, and then it was into the depths of Darlington shed for the second time that year. Forty six engines were on shed, with A1 60124 'Kenilworth' on standby duty. A number of Midland Region locos were waiting for attention at the works, but the J94 count was now down to just four. K1s and WDs vied for joint top place, number wise. I didn't do West Hartlepool this time, but hurried on to Sunderland, which was little changed from the year before, except the numbers were down. My plan was to do Heaton next, but something must have gone wrong, for I headed straight on to the two sheds at Blyth. In glorious sunshine, I strolled around the South shed, with fourteen J27s on, and headed across the water to the North shed. After writing down the twenty three numbers there, and noting that K1 2-6-0s were starting to encroach, I decided to do a bit of ship spotting. As I remarked earlier, I'd taken an interest in boats since my illness in February, and it was to pay big dividends this day. I had noticed some ships laid-up further along the estuary, and so I decided to investigate. As I walked along the outside of a wooden lath fence, out of the corner of my eye, I noticed familiar shapes. Without knowing it, I was walking past Hughes Bolckow's scrapyard, and those shapes were four A1s, withdrawn from Tweedmouth earlier that year. Numbers 60116 "Hal o' the Wynd', 60127 'Wilson Worsdell', 60132 'Marmion' and 60142 'Edward Fletcher', along with K1s 62003 and 62049 lay within the bounds of the yard. I copped three of the four A1s, and cleared all the class that were then in service. Incidentally, the ships were 'Corfoss', 'Cormount' and 'Arundel'. Once again, from the distance of forty years, it seems incredible that such news went unreported, but it was a different age, a slower culture. I noted three V2s as I passed Heaton depot, 60940, 60962, 60976. The first two were withdrawn from Gateshead, but 60976 lived on to work out of 64A, St Margarets, and was my only cop of the three. Also there were three J27s, numbers 65858, 65865 and 65879. Tyne Dock was the final port of call, containing just three classes, nine of which were 9Fs, five were J27s and ten were Q6s. It was then back to Newcastle, and home for 22.45, passing V2 60876 at Durham on a north bound parcels train at 19.56. The days of treble figure cops were now gone, for I only copped 38 that day.

Nowadays, people associate railway enthusiasts with anoraks and kagoules, but back then, I usually wore a blazer. An essential item was the scarf, and I usually wore the Riley High School one that had attracted the attention of the transport policeman on my visit to Immingham in February. It was always wrapped tightly around my throat, as I braved the howling gale that invariably confronted me when my head was out of the vestibule window. That is, in its normal position on a train trip. All weather protection was courtesy of the universal plastic pac-a-mac, which was very light, and could be rolled up into your pocket. I always travelled light, with one exception, a timetable. I learned very early, after a missed connection and no timetable with me, that you needed to think on your feet, and to be flexible. It was a pain carrying the massive Midland Region tome around, but it was essential. People today think that delays are a modern thing, but believe me, back then I can remember many trips were I had to turn around a twenty or thirty minute late arrival. I usually did this by totalling re-jigging the day, often reversing the order of the shed visits. For that, you needed very good time-tabling skills, and I often made decisions in a matter of two or three minutes, not hours or days. I still have the timetables that survived the rigours of the sixties, but not many of them are in good condition! It is rather spooky now to run my fingers over the tables that I used regularly, and sense the adventures that lay behind the bare letters and numbers on the browning pages. In those days, I knew off by heart all the numbers of the tables that I used regularly on my spotting trips, no matter what the region. Additionally, the duffle bag was generally considered de rigeur for the serious trainspotter, but I found that any spilled drink, or the folly of leaving it on the ground on a wet day, saw goodbye to the base. Therefore, my preferred mode of luggage was an ex-army canvas rucksack, which survived to the end of my trainspotting days. Another habit I picked up was the use of 'one trip only' note books. By that, I mean that I made small booklets out of scrap paper, large enough for making notes on one trip only. I'd lost a notebook at the end of 1963, and with it all my records for that year. I still had, and have, the records for the shed and works visits, with the exception of Darlington Works in November 1963, but all notes on numbers spotted en route vanished with the book. Furthermore, the next pocket book had survived a close encounter with a muddy pool, but only just. It survives to this day, but in tatters, and with a dark brown reminder of its unwelcome close encounter plastered all over the pages of the May 9th 1964 visit to the Western Region!

My third year at Riley High School was to start on Tuesday September 7th 1965, and as a last fling, I decided at short notice to visit the Manchester sheds on the Monday. Now, I don't know if the change of day from the more usual Saturday or Sunday or the lack of preparation had anything to do with it, but this wasn't a good trip. Don't get me wrong, every trip to see steam engines was a good trip, but this trip, like the one to Liverpool in February, just turned out badly. That is, I didn't achieve anything like I wanted to achieve, and I went home prematurely, feeling ill. Additionally, I left at the late time, for me, of 07.56. I recorded over twenty steam engines on the way to Manchester, the most notable being three Jubilees, 45573 'Newfoundland', 45593 'Kholapur' and 45597 'Barbados' on Holbeck shed. I visited Patricroft depot first, new territory for me. The shed held over thirty locos, with Standard 5 4-6-0s being the most numerous. Three Standard 3 2-6-2 tanks were present, 82000, 82009 and 82031, keeping 'Jinty' 47662 company. There followed another first, for I had not done Newton Heath shed before. This large shed in Northern Manchester was home to sixty steamers that day. Two local Jubilees, numbers 45604 'Ceylon' and 45632 'Tonga', along with Britannias 70017 'Arrow' and 70034 'Thomas Hardy' held pride of place. I then headed for Stockport, but something strange happened there. Despite it being familiar stamping ground for me, I took the wrong turning out of Edgeley station, for it had two exits, and got lost. I didn't feel too well, and so rather than regain my tracks, I called it a day and headed home.

Looking back, I think that I was just burnt out, for I tended to lose interest in railways after that, and pursue my other interests, ship spotting, particularly trawlers, astronomy and art. Like Ringo, I tried to 'Act Naturally', but something was missing, there was a space where the fire for steam locomotives had been. Maybe the impending demise of B.R. steam was beginning to sink in. Indeed, as Barry Macguire was singing about in the pop charts at the time, steam engines were on 'The Eve of Destruction', and with them the whole way of life that I'd known. Perhaps it was time to walk away, and follow The Walker Brothers advice to 'Make it easy on yourself' in the face of the inevitable. I usually had a list of target destinations, along with tentative times, on the drawing board. I would make up fantasy trips, and spend hours poring over timetables, but for the time being, that all seemed to fade away. Of course, I still kept an eye on the scrap line, and noted numbers down, but all plans for ' the next big trip' were shelved. A steady supply of 4Fs and O4s from South Yorkshire and the East Midlands arrived in September and October, and that alone kept the tally of steam engines that I had seen rising. On October 1st, I noted that 4F 44044 represented my four thousand five hundred and forty fourth cop! Apart from that, life went on, but drably.

Strangely enough, one of the school's history trips started to rekindle my interest. A trip to Coventry Cathedral was arranged for Friday October 29th. Once again, the school hired a private train, and at 08.25 on the appointed day, we rolled out of Paragon on a 'Magical Mystery Tour' of the Midlands. I noted over forty steam engines on the way. Our route took us via Selby, Gascoigne Wood and Pontefract Baghill to Rotherham, and then direct to Chesterfield, via Tapton Junction. We then continued via Burton and Nuneaton to the Cathedral City. My cops for the day were 48540 at Rotherham, 90722 at Chesterfield, 48552 at Burton shed, 45448, 48456, 46459, 78003 and 44866 and 48206, all while passing Nuneaton shed, and finally 46520 and 45017 at Coventry. After a sunny, but cold day looking around the town, we set off back in the dark at 18.00. Our return journey took us via Rugby Midland station, the only time in steam days that I visited the location. Here I copped 8F 48111. As it was pitch black outside, I only managed to record one more loco on the way back, 8F 48128 at Burton shed as we headed for home, arriving in Paragon station at 22.34. However, I'd only gone through the motions, doing what came naturally. That is, staring out of train windows, collecting numbers and muttering knowledgeably to lesser minions who had only recently caught the spotting bug. But there was no real fire for the sport. It took a bonfire night reunion with some old mates from Constable Street Primary School to fire up my enthusiasm once more. Until then, with this emptiness in my soul, I knew what The Beatles felt like when they sang 'Nowhere Man'.

Chapter 12

Day Tripper

Bonfire night 1965 was the turning point for me. I had a great time with some friends from primary school, twins Tony and Nick. However, after the thrills of the big night, and a lot of pocket money gone up in smoke, I felt very down the following day, as I desultorily poked the smouldering remains of the previous night's conflagration. 'A trip, that's what I need', I thought. Little did I know just how badly I needed that buzz once more, for I went straight home, dived into my bedroom, and pulled out my timetables once again. The intended target was to be just one shed, Colwick, for I was to ease myself back into the hunt again on the following Saturday, November 13th.

The day was cold but clear as I set off on the 09.00 to Sheffield Victoria. It was a late start for me, but it felt great to be striding across Sheffield to the Midland station. I arrived at Colwick & Netherfield station at 12.58, and was to spend just over three hours in the area. The depot, 40E (but soon to be 16B, although I didn't realise it at that time), held nearly sixty steam locos. K3 61943 was still hanging on as the stationary boiler, but the O4 2-8-0s had declined slightly to just seven representatives since the previous year. Thirteen B1 4-6-0s formed the major L.N.E.R. constituent, with nine 9Fs keeping them company. Twenty seven WD 2-8-0s graced the shed yard, and I saw a number more, along with three more O4s as I spotted by the crossing gates. Incidentally, Colin Gifford was in the area that day taking photographs, for I've seen several of his prints published that record the fact. With the light fading, I left the Nottingham area, and headed home with eighteen cops, but at least I was back once more!

I wanted to make up for lost time, so the next Saturday found Mike and I heading south to Bristol, or so we thought. At that time, I frequently found that the Midland cross-country services ran late, and so it was that day. Incidentally, one of the tricks that we used to pull involved the use, or abuse, of discounted tickets. In those days, day returns were not normally issued for journeys over sixty miles, and so we would string several together to get where we wanted to go, often racing out of at an intermediate station to book the next leg of the journey! Furthermore, any conditions on half-day excursions, and off peak tickets would be tested to the limit. We had the passion for steam, but not the purse to match! We were due to arrive in Gloucester at 11.26, bash the shed, and then on to Bristol for 13.18. That day, I couldn't make up for the time lost, and so the Bristol visit had to be aborted. As I mentioned earlier, after the Scottish shed bashing week, I was destined never to visit Bristol in steam days, for Barrow Road shed, 82E, closed to steam that very weekend. By way of compensation, there were three B1s at Rotherham for scrap, 61093, 61293 and 61299, but I copped none of them. However, we saw over twenty more steam locos on our journey down, and I copped a few of them, especially at Burton. Gloucester shed was a first for me. Mike and I got round, but as we stood at the crossing gates next to the shed, we saw several other spotters ejected by the foreman. It was late in the day for G.W.R steam, and so any location that promised their distinctive locos was fair game for the shed basher. There were 24 engine numbers there for me, the majority of which I copped. I was glad to add the two Midland 4Fs, 44264 and 44269 to my haul, but the G.W.R. influence was on the wane, with just one Hall 4-6-0, 6924, and two Manors, 7808 and 7816 present. A reminder of former glory days appeared later, in the guise of Castle 4-6-0 4079 'Pendennis Castle' on a special. I never saw a steam engine accelerate so rapidly as that train did out of Gloucester on that dull autumn day. It fairly flew out, as if in a final act of defiance against the new order, the diesel hydraulics that we had seen all day.

After it had departed we left the town, and with the light fading rapidly, we headed north, but not to Hull. We arrived in York at 20.24, or were due to, for the bare statement 'late' says it all in my notebook all these years later. 'Any time at all' was the motto for 50A, but we didn't do the full shed, for we had little time, and felt that the shed yard would be on the dark side. What we did see was still predominantly L.N.E.R. in origin, with 5 V2s, 3 J27s, 5 K1s, 7 B1s, and two of the final A1s, 60145 'Saint Mungo' and 60151 'Midlothian' on shed. I believe that 60151 worked the very last steam hauled train on the East Coast route that week, and was then withdrawn. It was probably the last time that I saw an A1 pacific in steam, for it was to be the A1s' last winter. I did see 60145 again, but only as a hulk at Draper's yard the following summer. The big surprise was a newly painted 0-6-0 that looked suspiciously like an L.M.S. 'Jinty', without its side tanks. Numbered cryptically as '2022', it had Mike and I scratching our heads, but not for long, as the 21.45 to Hull beckoned. The direct line via Market Weighton had one more week to go, but this wasn't to be the last time that I travelled on it. That privilege was to occur on the final day, Saturday November 27th. It transpired that the mystery locomotive, formerly 47564, and unfortunately not a cop for me, had been overhauled at Darlington Works for use at Holyhead Breakwater, not that we knew that at the time, for this was to be revealed several months down the line by 'The Railway Magazine'. The days of big cops seemed to be over, for I only copped twenty four that day, and it cost me over thirty shillings in travel! But how could you not feel good, with songs like The Who's 'My Generation' on the radio! I remember listening to Radio Luxembourg, and the pirate stations on a night, and it was always a thrill to hear new tracks and groups appearing on that fast moving scene. Alan Freeman's theme tune for his chart show seems to be indelibly etched on my brain, with the immortal words 'pop-pickers' bouncing around with it.

So we reach the final trip of 1965. The date was November 27th, and a heavy frost clung to the ground all day. Indeed, by the time I reached Market Weighton in the evening, it was snowing. Leaving Hull at 07.56, I travelled to Stockport via Stalybridge, using the short shuttle service between the two towns. Both Peckfield and Thornhill collieries still used steam power, and I would regularly see their tanks simmering in the early morning light. Jubilee 45626 'Seychelles' was stored on Holbeck depot, and its number joined the thirty other engines that I saw on my trip across the Pennines that day. Edgeley shed only had twenty locos on, with pride of place going to Jubilee 45596 'Bahamas'. The shed was still home to 'Crabs', with four on shed, and with just one, 42980, of the Stanier variety. Cop wise, I was rewarded more at Heaton Mersey across town, which held 24 engines. Here, there were no less than twelve of the Stanier 'Crabs', but an eye opener for me was a grubby 4F on the scrapline, number 44364. It was not in my Locoshed book, for I was to discover it had been withdrawn nearly two years before. Where had it been? Why had I not seen it on shed somewhere? Remember, the bush telegraph in those days was much more primitive. Ultimately, it transpired that it had been used as a stationary boiler at some carriage sidings, Guide Bridge, I believe. But it was a cop, and a very valuable one, having been withdrawn so long ago.

I had no intention of missing the last day of the York line, and so I headed back across the Pennines mid afternoon, arriving in the town at 17.02. It was dark by then, but I was still going to bash the shed, for this was York after all! Little had changed from the previous week, even down to the mystery 0-6-0. However, there were now four J27s lurking inside the shed, with two A1s just hanging on. To demonstrate the speed that I did sheds in those days, I left York on the 17.40 for Market Weighton! That's 38 minutes to get to the shed, do the roundhouses, run up the lengthy yard, back to the station, and buy a ticket! The train was hauled by Dairycoates B1 61306 hauling four coaches. I alighted at the sleepy Wolds town with snowflakes gently falling around me, and I watched the loco continue on its journey, first to Hull, and then ultimately into history, for it was to be preserved after withdrawal. As usual, I bought some tickets for my collection before pacing the platform to keep warm until I continued my homeward journey on the 19.38 train. The signalman must have taken pity on me, for he invited me into his signalbox. The warmth from the stove rolled over me as I entered this inner sanctum of railway operation. The railway worker seemed to have resigned himself to his impending fate, for it was one that was to be shared by many of his colleagues on the railways in the 1960s. I arrived home about nine o'clock, and within three hours, the direct Beverley to York line had gone.

Looking back, it wasn't just lines and locos that were disappearing. Of course, these were the images that fired the imagination, for they captured the sense of loss at the passing of the age. Steam engines were a visible, and when worked hard, a very vocal part of our heritage; for they lived, they breathed, they had a presence, they had a soul. Many of the lines, now long departed, had their devotees and regular patrons. Vociferous cries went up when closure was proposed. The petitions and placards came out and voices were raised, but it was all ultimately to no avail as the inevitability of events overtook the participants. Steam engines and unprofitable lines were potent symbols of a world that had perhaps outlived its time. But what about the smaller images that lurked on the fringes, and faded quietly away unnoticed, while our eyes were fixed on the giants of steam in their final swan song? In the 1960s, everyone realised that the water columns and the rusting braziers huddled beneath them were doomed to extinction along with the steam engine. I remember the ones on Manchester Exchange and Victoria stations the best. The smell of hot metal, the crackling of the tarry coal and the tang of acrid smoke comes readily to mind from winters past, as does the sound of the steady drip of cold water from the leather bag onto stone as the columns waited for their next customer. What wasn't so apparent was the loss of so many familiar features of the railway scene. There were Pullman cars, painted brown and cream, and with beautiful names, like 'Amethyst' and 'Opal'. My abc Combined Volume even had them listed, and so I collected them. They weren't steam engines, but they commanded respect. Stations had totem name signs in the appropriate colour for the region. Orange for the North Eastern, dark blue for the Eastern, green for the Southern, brown for the Western, maroon for the Midland and light blue for the Scottish region. Tickets were made of card, they always would be, wouldn't they? No, they, like platform tickets, have gone the way of the dodo and the steam engine. With great affection I remember the functional red machine, similar to a platform ticket dispenser, that stood on Hull Paragon station and was used to stamp out names on a thin metal strip. Fortunately, York Railway Museum still has one, and I can use it occasionally to sublimate my nostalgic urges! I even feel sentimental now about the first generation diesel multiple units, which all serious enthusiasts then disparagingly called 'bog carts'. They used to poison me with their fumes as I rattled my way towards a steamier destination aboard them, but at least I had a great view forward, and I could hang out of their sliding windows.

So 1965 drew to a close, with Draper's still carving up loads of engines, mostly 4Fs, WDs and 04s at that time, which was good for my cop count, but fatal for all the steam engines concerned. It was sad to see local hero, B1 61010 'Wildebeeste' on the scrap line on December 13th, but my abc combined volume now had 4629 steam engines underlined. The gaps in my book were getting less and less, but so was the tally of engines in service, for on the final day of the year, only 2980 steam engines were officially in service on the British national network. It had been a year when I'd travelled all over the country, with Scotland being the highlight. But there had been pain; firstly illness, then prosecution, and finally demotion to the B stream at my school. I had nearly lost my passion for steam, but I had regained it, stronger than ever. Yes, 1965 was the best of years, and it was the worst of years.

The year ended with The Beatles releasing 'Day Tripper', the ultimate shedbasher's song. It was to be my vestibule anthem from the very start of the following year, for 1966 beckoned, and it ultimately turned out to be the year that was to eclipse all my other trainspotting years in terms of travel and thrills. The music that year was terrific too!

Chapter 13

You won't see me

On December 3rd 1965, The Beatles released the 'Rubber Soul' album and my sister, Joan, played it practically non-stop that Christmas holiday. When she put any singles on, strains of the Beatles singing 'We can work it out' would drift through from the front room, which was appropriate, for I certainly could work it out, as I pored over timetables and locoshed books, planning my next master stroke. As always, Christmas was a good time for filling the coffers, ready for trips in the New Year. I was certainly going to need the cash, for the motto for 1966 was to be 'You won't see me', as I was to be away on train trips for more than fifty days that year! It all started off very low key, on January 2nd, with me as dead weight again, that is, sharing the petrol money, this time on the back of Mike's Honda 50. We had to wait until 09.00 for the frosts to clear, but then trundled off at 30 m.p.h. to the East Midland sheds of Langwith and Kirkby-in-Ashfield. By this time, the Eastern shed only had weeks to go before closure, and held 11 WDs, B1 61394 and three 'Coffee Pot' 2-6-0s. The old order was represented by just two O4s, 63612 and 63843. The neighbouring Midland shed was more promising with no less than 25 8Fs, three 9Fs, and 45406 with 90395 making up the final total of thirty locos. It was then a race against the clock to get back before dark. We didn't quite make it, for I stumbled off the bike at 16.40. I strongly recommend that under no circumstances do you repeat a similar 140 mile trip in January. I was only wearing my school trousers, shirt and school blazer, no leggings or padding. Therefore, I couldn't walk when I finally got off, but somehow I managed to crawl the fifty yards home from Mike's place. Luckily, my mam wasn't home, and I spread myself out in front of the fire to get some feeling back. When she got back I made out that everything was fine, but I think I was very lucky not to have suffered frostbite.

I went across to Ulceby a couple of times the following week, just for a lark with friends. Steam was still putting in regular appearances along the North Lincolnshire lines to Immingham, mostly in the guise of local WDs and 9Fs, but a Birkenhead example, number 92047, turned up on an oil train. My next 'real' trip was to Birmingham on the 15th. It was an icy day as I left Hull at 06.13. Chesterfield was taking quite a lot of locos for scrap at that time, and it held no less than five Midland 4Fs that day, one of which I copped, and a solitary WD, 90122. I was to do Saltley shed that day, but as usual the Sheffield to Birmingham train was late, and I made not one, but two miscalculations with buses. If I didn't know the area, such as Tyseley, I would ask the conductor (for they still had them in those days), to give me a shout when I got near. That was my usual practice, and it had served me well in the past. However, I obviously didn't trust the conductor on my bus, because I felt I was getting near, and then found that I had got off a mile early! The Spencer Davis Group, appropriately from the city, made number one the following week, and I then had to follow their advice to 'Keep on running', in this case through snow to the shed! It held 25 locos, with all the G.W.R. engines out of steam. There were four Granges, just one Hall, 6951 'Impney Hall', and a few panniers and 56xx tanks on, but 'Black Fives' now dominated the scene. At Wolverhampton, I made exactly the opposite mistake, for I got off the bus a mile late! The snow there was heavier, and it was even more of a trek back to the shed, 2B, or formerly, 84B. After passing under the distinctive arches that marked the entrance to the depot, the building was its usual miasmic clag-filled heaven, with 65 locos present. 'Black Fives' and L.M.S. 8Fs now held sway, but four Granges, and a motley collection of panniers represented the old order. Totally unexpected was the presence of not one, but two V2s, 60843 and 60923, which must have been on their way for scrap, along with Jubilee 45632 'Tonga'. In the final years of steam, almost anything could turn up at Oxley on its way to the scrapyard. These engines were often stored on the opposite side of the running line, and you needed to keep your eyes and ears sharp as you crossed to snatch those valuable numbers. I soon left that cathedral of steam, or rather a smoke filled cathedral, and headed for Bescot, just a few miles away. It held twenty five steamers, mostly 8Fs, with a few Ivatt 2-6-0s to keep them company. I copped 47 locos that day, but Saltley had been missed. Despite all the careful planning, it was mistakes that cost sheds, that's just the way it was. I might have just turned fourteen, but like The Beatles sang, and every serious shed basher knew, you had to 'Think for yourself'.

The snows were melting when I next ventured out on January 29th. It was first stop Crewe, with forty steam locos seen on the way. My notebook reminds me of two locos I saw as I passed Stockport Edgeley shed, 84019 and 84025. This Standard class was rendered extinct about that time, and it was rumoured that the engines gathered at the shed were due to go to the Isle of Wight to replace the ageing O2 tanks. It all came to nothing of course, but at that time we thrived on any rumours that kept the flame alive, even if only for a few more months. As usual, Crewe South was packed out, with over sixty locos present. Strangers in the camp were Jubilee 45593 'Kholapur' from Holbeck, and B1 61158 from Doncaster. Gone was the G.W.R. contingent, and gone too was Crewe North shed. It was then south to Shrewsbury, and with the snow melting rapidly in the noon day sun, I entered this shed for the second time in nine months. Nine Manors were in store, but pannier 9657 fussed past the shed as I recorded the 46 engines present. Two more Standard 2 2-6-2Ts, 84000 and 84004, lurked here as well. Along with three WDs, they were awaiting dispatch to their final resting place. Passing back through Crewe, I arrived at Stoke. This sprawling depot was home to over forty five locos. There were no surprises, but the trio of local 'Jinties', 47273, 47280 and 47307 were still active. With the light failing, I headed north to Stockport, were I arrived at 17.40, to bash the two local sheds in the dark. That was the benefit of solo travel, you had no one but yourself to consider. Dark sheds, and shadowy streets held no terrors for me, and soon I was crunching down Edgeley's cinder path, under the yard lights. Upon entering the smoky depot, I saw 45596 'Bahamas' hiding at the back of the shed, where it always seemed to be. Three more Standard tanks, 84013, 84017 and 84026, kept their classmates company on the scrap road. Mirfield WD, 90655, was a stranger, but Britannias, 70004 'William Shakespeare' and 70015 'Apollo', were local residents. It was then a bus ride out to Heaton Mersey shed, home to most of the remaining Stanier 'Crabs', for there were ten present. Wakefield WD, 90360, lodged peacefully among its L.M.S. 8F counterparts. I zoomed back to the station, where Fairburn 2-6-4T, 42116 hauled my Stalybridge train. A quick dash across the platform saw me catch the 19.55 'Trans-Pennine' unit back to Hull, home for 22.46, with 52 cops.

I was always keen to cop Western locos, and as I knew that the region, with the exception of the Somerset and Dorset, had been dieselised from January 1st, I set out for Worcester on February 12th. Mike came with me, and we hoped to catch the last of the

G.W.R stock before that inevitable trip to the breaker's yard. The journey was eventful, for we saw V2 60806 on a north bound freight at Doncaster, and then within five minutes, we saw classmate 60886 hauling passenger stock, as we rounded the curve onto the Sheffield line. Were we in 1966, or in 1963? The anachronism reasserted itself as we approached Sheffield, for on a scrap line, two miles north of the town, we saw a K3! It turned out to be 61943, from Colwick. By this time, it had been withdrawn over three years. That's how crazy the final years of steam were. Steam was still active on the Sheffield to Birmingham route, and we saw forty locos on the way. However, once again, the Midland cross-country route conspired against us, and we were late into New Street. We then shot off to Tyseley shed, and as Mike knew the right stop, there were no mistakes this time! There were less than twenty steamers on shed, of which only six were ex G.W.R. Pride of place went to 7029 'Clun Castle'. It was then a dash over to Saltley, with 36 locos on shed, mostly 8Fs, and quite a number of 9Fs. Incidentally, Saltley 9Fs seemed to get everywhere, it was that kind of depot. Snow Hill station beckoned for our trip out to Stourbridge. Even at this late date, three steam hauled freights passed through as we waited for our connection, two with 8Fs, and one with a 'Black Five'. We saw more steam power on the way, and 8F 48531 and pannier 9614 greeted us at Stourbridge Junction, as we approached the town. The shed was very run down by this late stage, but still held nearly thirty engines, mostly 8Fs and 'Black Fives', but there were several Standard types of the 76xxx and 73xxxx series. Five panniers were all that was left to remind us of the Great Western origins of the depot. That late train had cost us our Worcester connection, and so we went back to Birmingham. Like the Gloucester trip the previous November, I had been robbed of valuable Western cops by a very unreliable diesel service. It was no wonder that G.W.R. numbers were so valuable to me! For a reason that now escapes me, we then did Saltley for the second time that the day, which surely was a first! Maybe Mike and I were following Nancy Sinatra's advice that 'These boots are made for walkin'! We then headed back north, but I got off at Burton, leaving Mike to continue homewards, while I went off in search of more cops. Because my ticket didn't allow any break of journey, instead of leaving the station and pursuing the more usual route to the shed, I slunk off the end of the platform and went down the track and through the brewery yards to the depot. Imagine doing that today! There would be police everywhere, searchlights, and a chase, but the past was a different country. The shed held just fifteen locos, with WD 90437 visiting from Colwick, and B1 61035 'Pronghorn' from York. The obligatory shed 'Jinties', 47313 and 47643 were still hanging in there. I was home before ten, and I'd copped 33 numbers. This sort of figure was to be the norm in coming months, with one exception, a very big exception, in April.

On February 26th, I wanted to see, like The Beatles, 'What goes on', in the sheds of South Yorkshire and the East Midlands. As I turned left into St. Swithin Terrace on the approach to Doncaster shed, a plume of steam billowed over the bridge parapet. It was as though nothing had changed there since I first visited Doncaster in 1963. Dirty steam engines were still hauling equally dirty strings of coal wagons around the collieries of the area. What I didn't realise then, was that within six weeks, it would all be gone. I'd noted twelve locos on the journey from Hull to the town, and even copped one, WD 90075, in the station. The day had started well, and even at this final hour for Eastern Region steam, the shed held 54 steam engines, thirty of which were WDs, with seven B1s and nine 9Fs for company. The six O4s were on their last legs, and most appeared at Draper's yard within a matter of months. Canklow depot was next, with fifteen engines on. Nothing seemed that much different from my visit the year before, even though the shed had officially shut to steam the previous October! The three B1s, 61050, 61051 and 61315 were used for steam heating trains at Sheffield Midland station, but the tanks that were present were the eye opener. In the yard were Deeley 0-4-0Ts 41528 and 41533, Johnson 0-6-0Ts 41708, 41734, 41764, 41804 and 41835, and last, but not least, Kitson 0-4-0Ts 47001, which I copped, and 47005. A real menagerie in fact! I noted a number of withdrawn steamers at Chesterfield, including B1 61003 'Gazelle' and several other B1s. Westhouses only held eleven locos, but Midland 'Jinty', 47231 was still there, along with three 4Fs, which were to be among some of the last working in the country. Kirkby-in-Ashfield was still 8F city, but the big surprise of the day was Colwick. The shed was full to overflowing, with no less than 92 steam engines on, but gone was 40E, and in its place was 16B, for Annesley had just shut. The old order was out, with most of the L.N.E.R. engines on the scrap roads. Seven O4s, and nine B1s were there, but two B1s, departmentals No. 25 and 29 were in the shed. The smoke from over thirty L.M.S. 8Fs, and nineteen 'Black Fives' was drifting across the vast yard, and over the nineteen WDs which were now in store. Incidentally, like the Saltley 9Fs, Colwick 'Black Fives' seemed to get everywhere in 1966. As I soon read in the railway press, Colwick had been transferred to the Midland Region from January 1st. The world was changing fast, and it was now past the eleventh hour for Eastern Region steam. The Beatles could plead with me to 'Wait', but time was not on my side. At fourteen, I was a desperate boy on the run. I had to finish what I had begun in 1962. Like the Kinks, I was a 'Dedicated follower of fashion', but the fashion for steam was fast running out.

Chapter 14

Nineteenth nervous breakdown

It was March 1966, and The Rolling Stones were in the charts once more with 'Nineteenth nervous breakdown'. I'm sure that my mother would have exceeded that figure had she known all the stunts that I got up to on my travels! On March 5th I headed for Liverpool on the 06.50 'Trans-Pennine' train. After seeing forty engines on the way, Birkenhead was my first call. Over half the 37 locos on shed were 9Fs, but I was happy to see six 'Crabs' still active. It was a gloriously sunny spring day as I trudged into Croes Newydd shed. This depot was to be the last bastion of G.W.R. traction, and that day, eight panniers, and five 56xx 0-6-2 tanks were there to greet me. Chester shed was surprisingly empty at lunch time, with just nineteen engines on, mostly 'Black Fives' and Standard classes. I was little rewarded for the long bus ride out to Mold Junction either, for it only held fifteen locos, but at least I copped 9F 92203, later to be preserved as 'Black Prince'. I left Chester at the comparatively early time of 16.15, for I was going to drop off at Patricroft shed on the way home. There was a timelessness about the shed, which even now I can't put my finger on. No one was in view as I wandered around the ranks of the forty slumbering engines. WD 90456 from Frodingham was a long way from home, but it was never to return, even if it had wanted to, for the depot had been declared unsafe two weeks before, and all steam traction had now finished. The ranks of grimy engines were mostly Standard 5 4-6-0s, for which the depot was famous, and a number of 'Black Fives' and 8Fs. I left Patricroft at 18.15, and as it was getting dark, I saw little on the journey home.

So far, I have made light of the hazards of steam depots, but there were many, the most obvious being moving locomotives, but other potential threats existed. One such threat was the disposal pits, where engines dropped their fires. They were usually full of cinders and smouldering embers, but I never knew anyone who had fallen into one, or at least would admit to it! The final threat was more subtle. When writing down numbers, you never looked at the page, you always looked up at the engine numbers. No time was wasted, as you were always in a rush, always 'in between', and always on the wrong side of the law, so you kept an eye out for unsympathetic foremen. This left no eyes available for the washout points, which were like mines to the unwary. These sunken water cocks, recessed into the depot floor, were spaced evenly along the paths between the shed tracks. I never fell into one, but I had some near misses. You would be lucky if you only got away with a sprained ankle from falling into one, for they were about two feet deep! But there were also hazards away from depots. In those days, 'pea-souper' fogs were much more prevalent. It was on one such evening that my mate Brian and I went down to Dairycoates. After doing the shed, we crossed the main line on the embankment, then over the 'North Branch' goods line, and descended on a platelayers' hut. Here we made a fire and started to lark about. Now, unlike diesels, steam engines could be silent, just drifting along on a tiny whiff of steam. I ran out of the hut to be confronted by a WD's cylinder, less than two feet from my face! It was at the head of a rake of 16 ton open wagons, all empty, and coasting down effortlessly to the home signal, which neither crew member could make out in the fog. I froze as the steel giant ghosted past, with no sound but the gentle clink of the rear wagons buffering up just discernible in the distance. It was a close call, too close for comfort, for they couldn't have stopped, and would probably never have even known that someone had been run over. Visibility was measured in feet, not yards that night. It was no wonder that the fields were nick-named 'Foggy Fields'! Maybe I led a charmed life, or had nine lives like a cat, or just maybe I had a guardian angel, but I never fooled around on railway property again. From then on, it was stick to the basics, get to the sheds, get the numbers and get out.

The Manchester area was the next target, on March 19th. I saw Britannia 70050 'Firth of Clyde' at Leeds City, and copped classmate 70026 'Polar Star' on an east bound express freight at Stalybridge. Jubilee 45574 'India' was a class cop for me as I passed Holbeck shed. Three sheds, Trafford Park, Agecroft, with Midland 0-6-0 tank, 47202, and finally, Newton Heath fell in quick succession. This vast depot was home to five Britannias that day, and was well stocked with obligatory 'Jinties', holding four examples. WD 90126 was visiting from Wakefield depot, but everything else was par for the course i.e. 8Fs and 'Black Fives', with a total of forty seven engines present. I then trundled out of Central station and down to Buxton. This delightful location was a first for me, and the sun warmed my back as I walked briskly into the depot. Seventeen locos were present that afternoon, with the two J94 tanks, 68012 and 68079 being cops for me. Only two Midland 4Fs, 44271 and 44339, remained out of the fleet that the shed once boasted. I copped eight numbers on the shed, which by this date was more then I could cop on much larger sheds. It was then off to Stockport and the town's two sheds once more. They held few surprises by this date, but 'Bahamas' was missing, as were the 84xxxx series tanks from Edgeley depot. Twenty locos were at home, with two 'Crabs', 42712 and 42715 still hanging on. Heaton Mersey held thirty engines, mostly 8Fs, 'Coffee Pots' and Stanier 'Crabs', but WD 90707 was a visitor from Wakefield. It had been an Ardsley loco, but the depot had shut the previous October. The 19.35 to Bradford then beckoned, and it was the turn of Fairburn 2-6-4T, 42074, to haul the train. Not only was it a cop, but it gave a stirring performance across the Pennines, with cinders and smoke bouncing off the distinctive stone walls and tunnels that are a feature of the area. Too soon, I alighted at Huddersfield, and caught the comfortable, but soulless, diesel multiple unit back to Hull for 22.46, with 37 cops in the bag. Another great day, with the sun shining, and steam everywhere. The downside was the cinders that were in my eyes, for I always, without exception, hung my head out of train windows, so as not to miss any numbers. My mam bought me some plastic goggles, but I never wore them, for it was the sissy thing to do. I suppose that I could have got my block knocked off by a passing train, but as I'm here to tell the tale today, you can assume that that didn't happen. Talk about health and safety! However, as The Who were singing at the time, there was no 'Substitute' for the real thing - steam!

As you will have noticed, by this date, my trips were falling into a general groove of the Midland Region, largely in the North West and Birmingham area, but there were occasional forays to the North East, Scotland and the Southern. Steam was going fast, and the variety of previous years was declining rapidly too, for 'Black Fives' and 8Fs represented nearly half of all steam locomotives left in active service. April 1966 arrived, and once again, Mike and I hit the North Western trail, but this time with a difference. Firstly, it was my first trip for a while in the company of my friend Ian, and secondly, it was by hired car, a Ford Cortina Mark 2. Dave was to be our expert driver that day. This wasn't the Dave who had gone out with my sister, but a driver for the Fire Service! The month was marked by a considerable fall of snow, and we weren't confident that the trip would go ahead. Dave had laughingly remarked about taking a shovel the night before, and as requested, one was thrown into the boot on the morning of Sunday 3rd! We left Hull late, about 09.00, but Dave was a very hard driver with a fast car, and with the roads largely clear of traffic, we bashed eleven sheds in Lancashire that day! There was snow everywhere, but the sun was beaming down as Rose Grove, with 34 engines, became our first conquest. Three WDs from West Yorkshire were visiting, along with 9F 92017 from Carlisle. The next shed was the depot on the hill, Lower Darwen, but we were too late, for it had shut on February 14th. So it was 'No cops today, my allocation's gone away' to abuse the title of one of Herman's Hermits hits! Onward to Lostock Hall, which had 53 locos on shed. That was the great thing about Sunday shed bashing, loads of engines on shed. By this date, very few steam locos were rostered for passenger workings on a Sunday, and very few freight trains, apart from civil engineer's trains ran on the day. This meant all the more locos to grice in the grice mill! Numbers that stand out are Britannias 70017 'Arrow' and 70023 'Venus', along with York B1, 61319 and Royston WD, 90318. In quick succession we hit Springs Branch, with sixty engines on, the most notable being Britannia 70004 'William Shakespeare', and five of the remaining Stanier 'Crabs', then Sutton Oak, with twenty locos, and then Aintree. This shed was home to seventeen locos, six of which were 'Jinties'. Most of the sheds that day had their obligatory 'Jinty', but many were rationed to just one, so Aintree must have had a fondness for them! But there was no time to slow down. Edge Hill was next, which disappointingly only had thirty five on, but with a 'Jinty' tally of five. We then headed out of Liverpool, calling at Speke Junction. This site was more promising, with 45 steamers present. B1 61224 and WD 90409 were visiting from Wakefield, and 'Crab' 42765 had jogged across the Mersey from Birkenhead. We were now on the home leg, with Warrington Dallam revealing 23 locos. A brace of 4Fs still hung on there, 44294 and 44522, and WD 90126 had dropped in from Wakefield. The final shed was Bolton, with 49 engines lined up for our perusal. B1 61329 was a stranger from, you guessed it, Wakefield. Three Stanier 'Crabs' were on shed, with the remaining locos being 'Black Fives', 8Fs and a handful of Fairburn 2-6-4 tanks and Ivatt 2-6-0s. It was then back to Yorkshire for an arrival in the dark at 22.30. Despite the snow, the sun had shone all day, I'd copped 68 numbers, and we'd seen no less than 350 steam engines on ten sheds. Remember, all this had been achieved without a single mile on a motorway! The song for the day was 'Hold tight' by Dave Dee, Dozy, Beaky, Mick and Tich. It may have been a terrible name for a band, but that insistent opening guitar note made a career for them.

Riley High School had broken up for the Easter holidays, and so I chose the unusual day of Tuesday 12th to revisit the sheds of the West Riding. I had to use every opportunity to bash sheds, for I knew that there was a day coming soon when, like The Walker Brothers, 'The sun ain't gonna shine anymore' for all us steam fans. Leaving Paragon station at 06.50, I noted B1 61406 coming off Botanic Gardens depot, which had been dieselised in 1959. This was a regular feature during 1966, a B1 would often stable overnight there, and then go down to the station for train heating purposes. In fact, the only time that I bashed Botanic Gardens was when a B1 was on. I just wanted to do the shed for the score card's sake, and so I crept across the allotments in the dark, ran through the running shed, and back out into the dark. Anything for the buzz, and to underline the shed in my abc book! That day I did Manningham, with just eleven on, mostly 'Coffee Pots', and then Low Moor, which as its name implies, seemed a windy spot. There were twelve locos on shed, with Jubilee 45739 'Ulster' being the star. Gaining entrance to Holbeck by the hole in the wall, I was pleased to record five Jubilees there, 45574, 45593, 45660, 45675 and 45697. Also present among the twenty six engines was Carlisle Britannia 70053 'Moray Firth'. A short hop brought me to Wakefield, a much weightier proposition, with fifty five steamers on shed. Of course, the depot was WD city, with no less than 32 examples being present. The site was still home to Jubilee 45694, a handful of Fairburn 2-6-4 tanks and eight B1s, four of which were named. It was then time to mop up the smaller local depots, Royston, had fourteen on, and Normanton, with fifteen on, included Q6 63344, a stranger from Neville Hill. Finally, I just had time to fit in Stourton. This shed was a long bus ride out from the centre of Leeds, and its depths revealed a number of 8Fs, five 'Coffee Pots', and two visiting B1s. The three Standard 2-6-0s, 77000, 77003 and 77013, for which the depot was famous for, were also at home. With the final tally at twenty two locos on shed, I headed home with just 20 cops. Were the days of big cops over then? Like The Beatles on the Rubber Soul album, I firmly believed that 'The Word' was yes, but within days, I was to be proved wrong.

Chapter 15

Run for your life

In 1965, my father had joined Watergate Shipping Company of Newcastle, and in April 1966, as the captain of the 'Ravensworth', he arrived in Cardiff. I travelled down overnight to meet him on Friday 16th. There was little to see on the trip down, for it was dark of course, but I still sang my head off in the vestibule. Inappropriately, my anthem was 'Homeward Bound' by Simon and Garfunkel. I'd never done Derby motive power depot on my own, that is illegally, and I felt duty bound to bash the shed, with the cover of darkness helping. I gained access to the shed from the road overbridge at the south end of the station, by crossing the myriad of lines opposite the depot. The shed held just twenty two steamers, including B1 61237 and Britannia 70047, but at least all was quiet. That is, until I went back across the tracks. A tannoy boomed out 'stay were you are', and fearing that I was to be done for trespassing once more, I decided, like The Beatles, to 'Run for your life'! It was the witching hour of midnight, and I ran back to the station and hid in any coach that I could find until my train for South Wales arrived. It may have been hauled by 'the enemy', a 'Peak' diesel, but I was glad to be out of Derby and ambling south via Birmingham New Street, where it seemed to stay for ages. The train then went via Worcester, where I noticed a couple of steamers simmering on shed, but couldn't get their numbers, and on to Cardiff. I arrived there at about 06.00, and set out for Barry Docks. Mike had visited there the previous summer, on a trip that I would have dearly loved to have accompanied him on, but couldn't afford, and he reported a large build up of engines. In my heart, I expected that cutting up would have commenced, and that the backlog would now have disappeared. As my D.M.U. rattled around the curve into Barry, a sight reminiscent of Darlington Works, but on a much grander scale hove into view. Southern and Western locomotives were lined up in sidings and on embankments as far as the eye could see. So it was true, Barry was becoming a Shangri-la where my beloved steamers were coming home to die! Remember, information spread much more slowly in those days, and one didn't always believe it when you finally read it. 'Daydream' was a hit at the time for The Loving Spoonful', but Barry had now gone from a daydream to reality! It was just after seven on a Sunday morning, and with no one in sight, I vanished like a ghost among the rusting hulks. There were one hundred and fifty five locos there that day. It would be tedious to list them all, and the ranks of these 'undead' are too well known to be worth repeating, but I did cop one hundred and fifteen of them! The big cops were back in town! Not only that, but I always valued long withdrawn cops most of all, and some of these had been withdrawn as long ago as 1959. Mentally I'd written these engines off, for you usually had a second chance to see active locos again, or so you hoped, but for the dead there were no second chances. It was then back to Cardiff, and off to the docks to see my dad. He was glad to see me, but the first officer less so, for I'd been the pest that had had his head out of the window all the way past Severn Tunnel Junction and Newport, keeping him awake!

My dad was due to take over another ship in London, and so we left the 'Ravensworth' that afternoon. The taxi stopped at East Docks Depot, just for me, but all its tracks were clear of steam locos by that date. With my dad paying, we travelled first class to Paddington. I managed to grab a few numbers passing Newport and Severn Tunnel Junction, but all the remaining depots to London were steam free. By the evening of Sunday 17th, I was going aboard a ship in East India Docks. On the Monday, I spent a couple of hours spotting at Waterloo, but the time was better used on Tuesday, as I went down to the South Coast. I was still copping quite a lot of numbers on the Southern, for I gained no fewer than nine on the way to Bournemouth, with 'Black Five' 44710 of Banbury shed in Central Station. 70F held about twenty five locos, and I copped another nine here. I then journeyed west, but my luck ran out, as a late train sabotaged the day. I did get to Weymouth, but not in time to do the shed. That privilege would have to wait until September. Appropriately, in view of my night-time maritime abode, Merchant Navy 35010 'Blue Star' hauled me back to Eastleigh, which amazingly only had twenty three steamers on shed, and that included preserved M7 30053 and 'Schools' 4-4-0 30926 'Repton'. 'Black Five' 45418 was an interloper from Banbury. Now luck can be a two way thing, for on the train to Eastleigh was another spotter, and he'd done both Newport and Severn Tunnel Junction depots the previous weekend. This gave me the valuable opportunity to extract nine more numbers, five of which I copped, from my South Wales bash.

The sharing of information like this was typical of the camaraderie between train spotters in the 1960s. In fact, most of the larger stations had enthusiasts hanging around platform ends who were only too willing to share information. It was then back to Waterloo behind Standard 5 73088, copping four more on the way.

The following day, I went into town with my dad and visited Clapham Museum, which held fifteen preserved locomotives, but I wanted to be on the move once again, and so I left my dad in the capital, and headed out to Oxford. There were still twenty seven steam engines stored on shed, and I copped many of them. Most were Halls and Modified Halls, but two Granges, 6849 and 6872, kept them company. WD 90258 was a long way from its home at Langwith, but it had either failed there, or it was stored. Either way, it was never to go home, for 41J had shut in February, and so its fate was already sealed. Looking back, I lost an opportunity that day, for Banbury depot, only 25 miles away, was still active, and I never got to do it in steam days. Once again, the G.W.R. jinx, c'est la vie! On my final day in London, I spent a pleasant three hours on Waterloo Station, but didn't cop anything. It was then back to the ship, and a midnight departure from East India Dock, bound for Hull. I stayed on the bridge for a while, but awoke the following morning off the Norfolk coast. We arrived in King George Dock after eight in the evening, and then it was home to bed, with no less than 207 cops to mark in my abc from my seven days away!

On Saturday April 30th I noted that the tracks were still down at Hornsea station, but more distant and active destinations beckoned on Sunday May 1st. It was off to the North West once more, and the remaining Manchester sheds. My only cop on the way was WD 90694, which later gained the unofficial name 'Falaba', at Huddersfield depot. First shed was Newton Heath, with seventy three locos on, including its last Jubilee, 45654 'Hood', and four Britannias. Next was Trafford Park, home to a number of Fairburn 2-6-4 tanks and a solitary Fowler example, 42334. There were thirty locos present, but at least this was more than the twenty four on Agecroft. The depot was to close in October, and its decline was evident. Johnson 'Jinties' 47201 and 47202 hung on, but 8F 48539 reflected the shed's fate, for it had been badly damaged in an accident, with the tender taking the brunt of the collision. Patricroft shed was home to forty four steamers, and 8F classmate

48181 had also been in the wars, for it had lost its chimney! Britannias 70034 and 70051 kept company with withdrawn WD 90456, the Frodingham loco that I'd seen in March. It was then back to Manchester Exchange station, which I knew so well, for it was the starting off point for so many of my adventures in the North West in those final years of steam. I have fond memories of standing under the large clock at the western end of the station at the end of a hard day's spotting, usually waiting for the 18.43 or 19.43 D.M.U. back to Hull. It was famous for possessing the longest platform in Britain, and many's the time that I walked along it to Victoria station. However, its celebrity status didn't stop it disappearing from the railway map immediately after steam finished. On the way home I dropped in at Holbeck depot, which held twenty seven locos, including four Jubilees. It became a regular feature of my North West forays to bash this shed any time I passed through Leeds. It was back to business as usual, for I only copped eighteen that sunny Sunday.

Draper's yard was cutting up WDs big style at the time, and many of the withdrawn Eastern Region examples were now heading Hull-ward, but I was soon heading off to the Midlands. The Mamas and The Papas could sing about 'Monday, Monday', but I lived for Saturday, and in this case, May 7th. Chesterfield scrap yard was home to no less than six B1s and a solitary WD, 90516. Despite the heavy dieselisation of the Derby area, I still noted six steam engines as I passed the shed on my way to Leicester. The shed 15A was due to close to steam in June, and only nine steamers were present, 48082, 48165, 48381, 48530, 48671, 78013, 78021, 78028 and 78061. The Standards were kept for the Desford branch, but they were still to go the following month. Next was my first, and last, visit to Nuneaton, which had twenty six on shed. Like Leicester, it was due to close in June, but you would never have guessed it, for the area was alive with steam, mostly 8Fs. I copped eight there, which was good by that late stage in the game. However, I managed to beat that tally at Saltley, but only just! Considering that the visit was within the last ten months of steam in the area, it is nothing short of miraculous that the depot held fifty six engines, most very much in steam. Dairycoates regular, B1 61012, was a long way from home, but the rest, apart from a few Standards, were mostly 9Fs, 'Black Fives' and 8Fs. A quick trip across the city brought me to Tyseley, home to twenty six engines. The G.W.R. was represented by Castle 7029, panniers

3625 and 9774 and Prairie tank 4176, the remainder being 9Fs, 'Black Fives', with a few Ivatt 2-6-0s. I travelled back to Doncaster, noting that Burton had lost its 4Fs, but gained York K1 62042 as a visitor. Doncaster was to be the surprise of the day, for all the steam locos were stored, apart from Holbeck Jubilee 45593 'Kholapur', which was collecting some of the last coal from the coaling stage. Thirty seven locos, and only one in steam. So steam on the Eastern Region had drawn to a close, only weeks after the Western Region had declared itself 'steam free' upon the closure in March of the much loved Somerset and Dorset line. This was bad news indeed, and although I had copped 26, the gloriously sunny day ended with a tinge of sadness. During May, The Rolling Stones reached number one with 'Paint it black', and my mood soon reflected that of the song. The inevitability of it all was beginning to dawn on me, and it hurt, but this was no time to grieve, for time was short, shorter than anyone realised then.

My dad's ship was in dry dock at Smith's yard at North Shields, and this gave me the chance to travel by car with him the following weekend. I dropped in on the Blyth sheds, the South shed only holding six engines, all J27s. 'Coffee Pot' 2-6-0s 43101 and 43132 were a new departure for the North shed, and K1s were starting to nudge the J27s out. Bolckows scrap yard held nine locos, 61188, 61248, 63371, 63389, 65805, 65821, 65844, 65851 and 92179. The Q6s and J27s were local, but the others came from the Nottingham area. However, I copped nothing from this visit, and I had to wait until a visit to the North West on May 21st to gain any more numbers. About this time, another spotter appeared on the horizon, also called Phil. Like many others, he promised to go on trips with me, but, to my recollection, he never did. Few had the commitment to chase the last of the 'steam dragons', but I had, and no one was going to hold me back.

A brilliantly sunny May 21st found me leaving Paragon station on one of my regular trains, the 06.50 to Leeds, destination Carnforth. My first port of call was Skipton, with fourteen locos. The Midland 4Fs had gone, but the depot was still home to three 'Jinties', and a stranger from Hull, WD 90704. Six Standard 4 4-6-0s, which were to become a feature of the area in the shed's final months, kept Britannia 70003 'John Bunyan' company. I dropped off at Hellifield station, which appeared very run down, and slunk across the line to peer into the abandoned shed. There was a crack in the door just big enough to make out 4F 44027 and V2 60800 'Green Arrow', which was a cop for me. It was then on to a new location for me, 10A. The shed, so clearly visible from the station platform, held over forty steamers, all regular L.M.S. fare, with two visiting Britannias, numbers 70009 and 70039. Despite it being a new conquest, I only copped five numbers there, for Carnforth locos tended to get all over. Incidentally, the day was to have included Lancaster Green Ayre shed, but I'd got wind that it had just shut in April, so I missed the county town and headed for Lostock Hall. The forty three engines on shed included Britannia 70018 'Flying Dutchman', 'Jinties' 47293 and 47336, and following me from Hull, WD 90352! But there was no time to waste, for I was off to Blackburn, and Rose Grove shed. It was a nice to see nearly thirty locos, all 'Black Fives' and 8Fs, quietly smoking away in the shed yard, but personally it was a blank, for I copped none. As was my custom, I bashed Holbeck on the way home, but again I scored nil points. Old timer Q6 63387 was in steam as I passed Neville Hill depot, for it was probably getting ready for one of the Civil Engineers' Sunday specials that kept these veterans in regular work in the Leeds area. I arrived home at 21.19, with seventeen cops in the bag. The Troggs could have been singing about me with their first single, for I was a 'Wild Thing' in the spring of 1966, chasing steam engines wherever they still remained.

Chapter 16

Paperback Writer

On May 28th, I did something unusual, I actually spent hours on a station just watching freights pass through! The station was Wakefield Kirkgate, and I did nip over to see the fifteen engines at Normanton about tea time, as well as bashing 56A twice that day. I saw 59 steam locos pass through the station in the space of six hours, including a treble header with WDs 90405, 90210 and 90417 in charge. By the evening, 56A held sixty six steamers, which included no less than forty nine WDs! I only copped three numbers that day, but those pleasant few hours were still a delight to my young eyes.

At this time, my dad was captain of a ship that was in Smith's dry dock at North Shields. Unfortunately for the shipping companies, but fortunately for me, the British seamen had gone on strike. This meant that when the necessary work was completed on the ship, there was no way that it was leaving the yard. Therefore, as spring turned to summer, I spent a few days on the ship with the family. On May 30th I dropped in at Tyne Dock depot, which was still home, if a rather derelict one, to eight 9Fs, and eleven Q6s. It seemed surprisingly empty for a Bank Holiday Monday. The next day, I travelled up to Alnmouth, as the line to Alnwick was due to close anytime. What a delightful little sub shed that was. It held two locomotives, K1 62021, which I copped, and V2 60836, from Dundee, no less, but I didn't cop it. The V2 was actually hauling the branch trains, but what brought it that far south at this late stage will always remain a mystery to me. The weather was beautifully sunny all the time I spent on the Tyne, and on June 1st I did Heaton motive power depot. The depot had closed to steam in June 1963, but continued to repair steam engines until the end in September 1967. It was the first time that I had bashed the shed, and I was pleasantly surprised to find nine locos lurking there; J72s no 58 and 59, K1 62011, which I copped, and companion 62027, Q6s 63406 and 63453 and J27s 65815, 65861 and 65892. I then did the short hop to Sunderland, which held only ten locos, but it was a weekday, and at least I copped 63346. Changing direction, I went back to Newcastle, and retraced my steps to Alnmouth again. 60836 was still hauling the local trains, but 62057 was now on shed.

I enjoyed my few days up in Geordie Land, but it was then back home, and back to the serious business of concerted shed bashing. Dusty Springfield could well sing 'Going Back' that month, for I would have loved to have gone back in time to see more steam locos, but I had to content myself with going back on June 4th to the Liverpool area, which was still very steamy. Once again the 06.50 to Leeds was my chosen mode of transport, and I saw about forty steamers on my way to Wigan. I copped B1 61199 opposite Neville Hill, and noted Britannias 70051 at Holbeck and 70012 at Manchester. Springs Branch only held thirty eight locos, of which I copped two. It was then off to the coast for my one and only visit to Southport depot. This was a very timely visit, for the shed closed the following Monday! It only held ten locos, mostly Fairburn 2-6-4 tanks, and 'Black Fives', but 47566 kept up the tradition of the obligatory Jinty. I copped two there, and then it was off to Birkenhead, which was home to thirty nine engines, with six 'Crabs' mingling among the throng, mostly 9Fs, and three 'Jinties' thrown in for good measure. WD 90678 was a visitor from Wakefield. It was then under the Mersey and into Edge Hill, home to thirty seven engines, including three Jinties and several Stanier 'Crabs'. I dropped in on Newton Heath on the way home, which held no less than sixty three steamers. All was the usual L.M.S. fare, apart from B1 61131, again from Wakefield, and the cop of the day for me, long withdrawn 4F 44246. I have no idea where it had been hiding for the previous year! I arrived home at 21.19, having paid Holbeck a quick visit. I managed to cop 25 numbers that day, which was a good tally by this late date.

The Beatles released 'Paperback Writer' the following week, and I would never have guessed it then, but forty years later, that is what I would be doing! My mate Brian came with me on my next outing, which was to Manchester on June 18th. Naturally we did Holbeck on the way home, with 70016 visiting. One of the last Fowler 2-6-4 tanks 42394 was on shed, but only two Jubilees, numbers 45660 'Rooke' and 45697 'Achilles' were present. Additionally, we visited Huddersfield depot, which was home to only nine locos, mostly WDs. We spent three hours on Manchester Exchange Station, noting over thirty steam locomotive movements, but then it was off to one of those hallowed steamy dens: Newton Heath, home to fifty two locos, including doyen of the Britannias, number 70000. Incidentally, 44246 was still hanging on there. A short train ride brought us to Patricroft, with thirty five on, including 'Crab' 42727 visiting from Birkenhead. 9J, Agecroft, was fuller than usual when we visited it at tea time, with thirty four engines present. Johnson 0-6-0Ts 47201 and 47202 still hung on precariously, but the end for the shed was only four months away. We got back home at 22.46, but I copped just six locos that day, that's all.

I planned to go to Scotland on my own when the summer holidays came, and to that end I started saving, writing off to bed and breakfast places, and last but not least, ordering my railrover ticket. I started bus spotting at this time, and biked everywhere locally to collect them, but it hardly had the fascination of spotting living, breathing locomotives. Plenty of engines were now wending their way to Draper's Yard, and steam was still fairly common on summer excursions, mostly 'Black Fives' and B1s. However, I didn't notice any steam engines on Bridlington shed that year, and I now realise that they went up to Scarborough depot for servicing between turns. In July, one of the last A1s, 60124 'Kenilworth' arrived on the Dairycoates scrapline. So Monday July 25th arrived and I set off for Scotland, via Carnforth. As usual, it was a sunny day, and 10A was home to thirty six engines, but I copped none. 44905 then hauled my 11.11 Carlisle train to Oxenholme. To give an idea of how tight I used to schedule the shed bashes, I only arrived in Carnforth at 10.46. That's 25 minutes to do the shed, and get a ticket for the north! I was off to Tebay depot, which I'd never done, but I had to use a bus from Oxenholme to get there, and I remember a long wait in the scorching sun. I had copped 42210 and 44838 near Oxenholme, and a further five locos were to follow on this delightful little shed, which was home to 42110, 42154, 42225, 43009, 43029, 43033 and 44907. It was then off to Workington, via Carlisle. Again, I'd never bashed this shed, and I copped six of the fifteen engines present. The long time residents, ex M.R. 4Fs, had now gone, and replaced mostly by 'Coffee Pot' moguls. Carlisle Kingmoor was still steam city, with eighty six steamers dozing on shed that evening. There were thirteen Britannias present, with one of the last Clans, 72006, and York B1 61035 keeping them company. Upperby was home to twenty locos, and it was here that I copped my last Britannia, 70048. I'd copped twenty two numbers the first day of my holiday, which was to be nearly half of my total for the whole four days away. It was then back to my digs for the night, where I rang my mam to tell her I was alright.

The next day I was off over the border. I jumped off the train at Dumfries and ran like hell, for I'd allowed myself six minutes, yes six minutes, to bash the depot! However, the shed had closed in May, and was home to a solitary 'Black Five', 45480, but at least I copped the loco. Hurlford depot held only eleven engines, and I only copped 77017. Ayr was more promising, with thirty engines, with no less than ten being 'Crabs'. I copped three Standards there, and then it was off to Glasgow. Eastfield was home to fourteen engines, including A4 60034, but WD 90468 was the cop for me. Perhaps put off by the threatening atmosphere the previous year, I skipped Polmadie, and headed for Motherwell. There were nineteen steamers on shed, with pride of place taken by A2 60528 'Tudor Minstrel'. It was then back to Glasgow for Corkerhill. The depot was home to twenty eight locos, which was a large tally for a Scottish motive power depot at this late date. I copped two there, 73009 and 45488. There were a number of visiting locos from Carlisle, and Standards formed the majority of the allocation. It was then back to my digs, and the obligatory call home to please my mam. Remember, I was still only fourteen!

On the Wednesday, I headed for Perth, with twenty one engines on shed, including A4 60026 'Miles Beevor', and Britannia 70003 'John Bunyan'. However, my cops were much more mundane, 44997 and 80093. Dundee was home to fifteen locos, with all being ex L.N.E.R stock, apart from two 'Black Fives'. Once more, I copped two here, before I tackled Thornton Junction. Again I copped just two numbers here, 65920 and 65925, but at least this large sprawling depot held a creditable thirty seven steam engines. Old timer J36 65345 was still doing sterling service as the depot stationary boiler. Heading south through Fife, Dunfermline was my next port of call. I copped just one loco, 65930, among the seventeen engines on shed. My digs were to be the Y.M.C.A in Edinburgh, and so before settling down for the night, I went to St Margarets shed, always a favourite of mine. However, the tally of locos was just the same as at Dunfermline shed, which was much smaller, seventeen. I copped 60955, one of the four V2s present. A final call at Waverley Station proved fortuitous, for not only did I cop V2 60919 on a Dundee train, but another spotter told me what locos were dumped at Troon scrapyard, which I'd passed the previous day. They were 42148, 42179, 42676, 42909, 45182, 45471, 46450 and 47676. I copped the 'Jinty' and the Ivatt 2-6-0.

My railrover ticket was obviously for seven days, but I actually only spent three days in Scotland, probably due to lack of funds, parental constraints, or the mistaken belief that I would complete all the Scottish numbers that I needed, or perhaps because of all three! My final day started well, for I copped 45492 at Waverley Station as it came off a Carstairs train. Additionally, ex works A4 60024 'Kingfisher' was in steam at Eastfield and was a class cop for me, but classmate 60004 'William Whitelaw' ultimately eluded me. There were tales that after the mishap with the crossing gates that led to its withdrawal, it was dumped at the back of Perth shed, but I never saw it there. I quickly dropped in at 67A, Corkerhill, before travelling out to Carstairs. The shed only had fourteen steamers present, but I copped 76090 and 45309. It was then back to Edinburgh, were I copped 45053 as I passed St Margarets shed, on my way to my last shed bash of the holiday, Tweedmouth. This was the only time I did this small depot, and amazingly, it was also one of the few occasions when I've been thrown out! The shed had closed to steam in June, and was home to K1 62006, which I copped. At least the gentleman who was responsible for my removal was helpful, for he informed me that it was due to go to Cowlairs for scrap! However, I think he was mistaken, for at this late stage, no B.R. works were cutting up locomotives, all went to private yards. As word travelled so much more slowly then, I was amazed to see Darlington depot empty on my way past, for I was unaware that it had shut completely in March, along with the works.

So I trundled home with fifty cops under my belt, all for the cost of £7 / 14 / 1d! The very last A1, 60145 'Saint Mungo' was in store at York depot, and was to make its sad journey to Dairycoates, and then Drapers, in August. Things were changing, for my Gala pies cost 10d that holiday, compared to 9d the previous year! However, much bigger changes were afoot, for the day I arrived home, July 28th, Chris Farlowe and the Thunderbirds reached number one in the pop charts with 'Out of time'. With only two years to go before steam went completely, I too was running out of time.

Chapter 17

Here, there and everywhere

On August 5th 1966, The Beatles released their album 'Revolver', and I decided to take their advice and travel 'Here, there and everywhere' the following day. I was off to Holyhead, a place that I had never visited. The sight of two Jubilees, 45562 and 45647 double heading empty coaching stock opposite Neville Hill, was a thrill to see and two 2-6-4 tanks, 42152 and 42271 busied themselves on station duties at City station. Yes, 55H might have shut to steam in June, but Leeds was still a very steamy place. I arrived at Manchester Exchange at 09.56, and caught the 10.20 to Llandudno Junction, which was hauled by Britannia 70041 'Sir Henry Moore'. I copped a couple of locos passing Chester shed, but saw little along the North Wales Coast. Arriving at 6G slightly late, I rushed around the depot, which held just eight engines, 44772, 44807, 44971, 45064, 47673, 73073, 73094 and 73139, none of which I copped. This was not good, and worse was to follow! The 13.26 to Holyhead immediately proceeded to lose time, and as I had only allowed twenty minutes to bash 6J, I abandoned ship at Caerwen, and waited for a Chester bound train to take me homeward. As I mentioned in an earlier chapter, this demonstrated the importance of carrying a timetable to allow for drastic changes at very short notice. I copped just five that day, and it was an expensive trip, but then you win some, you lose some.

Looking back, I often wonder if I'd have enjoyed the steam scene so much if it had been destined to last for many more years. I have to be honest to myself and say no. The thrill of the chase and the race to see as many steamers as possible in the limited time available gave it that buzz. Certainly I would have enjoyed watching them at work, but without the sense of imminent extinction, I think it would have all been a little less exciting. Anyway, back to 1966! That summer holiday, as in the previous ones, I spent a great deal of time at Dairycoates shed, noting 60145, 'Saint Mungo', the last of the A1s, on the scrap line on August 9th. Most of these jaunts were with my mate Brian, and we would often resort to train spotting from 'Foggy Fields' after our visit. We'd sometimes spend all day there, watching engines hard at work. They would often set fire to the embankment with their sparks, and I can remember Brian and I waving frantically at passing trains to warn them of the dangers ahead. In our minds we could see conflagrations, warped rails, derailment and disaster, but the train crews had seen it all before, and just chugged past. It was all very 'Railway Children', but I think we were more likely to be sworn at than rewarded for our supposed gallantry!

On Sunday August 14th, with strains of The Kinks 'Sunny afternoon' on the radio, I was off on a coach trip run by a local trainspotting society to the Crewe and Manchester areas. We left at 06.15, and our party was bunking Patricroft before 10.00. For some reason, we made a note of a line of engines at Newton Heath, but didn't actually do the shed. I assume that the tour guide did not possess a pass for that depot. By this time, I tended to cop just one, or occasionally two locos per shed, and indeed that was the pattern for the day. 9H held 46 locos, mostly Standards, 9J, Agecroft, just 31 and 9B, Stockport Edgeley, 41. It was then on to Crewe South, home to no fewer than 87 steamers. I managed to cop all of four locos there! It was a 'sunny afternoon' as we strolled around the works. Steam activity was winding down, and only 30 engines were present. A4 60007 'Sir Nigel Gresley' took pride of place, but my only cop was the humble works shunter, 4F 44525. The vast depot at Stoke was our next destination, and was home to 54 locos. I copped three here, including my last extant 'Coffee Pot', number 43088. Some discussions must have then taken place, for an unscheduled stop was made at Buxton, and despite the lack of a permit, thirty spotters tiptoed around the shed to see the 22 engines housed there. It was then home for 22.50, with just thirteen cops in the bag.

I don't know where the money came from, but the following week I started a seven day Northern Railrover. This ticket covered all of England north of a line from Doncaster to Crewe, and therefore covered most of the area still using steam power. The ticket commenced on Thursday 18th, when I visited 9B, 9E, 9F, 9K and 8F, and I copped nine, two of which were on Springs Branch, home to 38 locos. There was plenty of steam to be seen, 34 on Bolton, 22 on Trafford Park, 36 on Stockport Edgeley and 20 on Heaton Mersey. The next day proved to be very poor indeed, with only three cops. First stop was Birkenhead 8H, with only 25 steamers on, and Aintree 8L with a mere 9 locos present. The first blood was drawn at Bank Hall 8K, when I copped 'Black Five'

45386 among the 17 engines there. Edge Hill 8A was home to 33 engines, and a further cop of 92078. Speke Junction 8C held only 22 engines, and Warrington Dallam 8B, even fewer, at just 16. Even the mighty motive power depot at Newton Heath, 9D, home to no less than 58 steam locomotives drew no further cops. Incidentally, A2 60532 'Blue Peter' was on shed there, obviously in connection with some rail tour, and WDs 90112 and 90417 were visiting from Wakefield. The final cop of the day came near Dean Lane station with 8F 48731. A smile crossed my face as I passed Huddersfield shed, for they had unofficially named another WD, 90680, for it sported the name 'Ionio' in yellow on its side. So it was home with only three cops under my belt. The truth was that I was now mopping up the last one hundred engines that I could potentially cop. Additionally, the variety had all but disappeared. There were only two ex Midland 4Fs working, and they were the Crewe Works shunters, and even the humble 'Jinty' was now a delight to see.

The following day was better, with visits to Carnforth, Lostock Hall, Heaton Mersey and Stoke. What an eclectic tour, but what the hell, I had a rover, so there was no additional cost to this wacky itinerary! Standard 77000 was shunting at a power station near Armley, as I sped past on my way to Carnforth 10A. I copped two there among the 41 locos on shed. Lostock Hall was home to 33, with just one cop, before I travelled down the West Coast main line to Crewe. Even at this late stage of the game, I saw no fewer than 53 steamers between Preston and Stoke! This included two WDs, 90620 and 90625 from Wakefield at Preston. Obviously workings from the West Riding still brought regular steam turns across the Pennines. Stoke MPD was home to 33 locos, but with only one cop, 75032. I then continued home via 9F, were amazingly I copped two locos, 44725 and 48612, despite only doing part of the shed! On the Saturday I once more attempted to crack the North Wales coast. Wisely, I allowed from 14.28 to 16.00 at Holyhead to bash the shed! I noted over fifty steam locomotives on the way to Llandudno Junction, where once again I drew a blank cop wise out of the nine steamers at home. I copped just three that day, and all of them were in the Holyhead area, 45247, 47410 and 44770. 6J held twelve engines, with Britannia 70023 'Venus' top of the list.

My mother was still a force to be reckoned with, for I was due to visit the Newcastle area on the Sunday, but my mam put her foot down 'because it was raining'! After all, I was still only fourteen, and I suspect that the source of finance for the whole jaunt was from her. The best made plans of men and mice can come to nothing, or as The Beatles put it, 'Tomorrow never knows'! That didn't stop the trip on Monday, when I noted J27s 65809 and 65811 at Selby on their way to Hull for scrap. I was due to bash several depots that day but had to abandon some of them as train times went adrift. However, I did manage Shrewsbury, 6D, courtesy of an extra ticket that cost me an arm and a leg! At least I copped three there, out of 30 on shed. Croes Newydd 6C still held several pannier tanks in steam, but I only copped 48147 out of the 14 locos on shed. It was then off to Birkenhead, home to 32 steamers, but I only copped 8F 48035. Crossing the Mersey, Aintree held just 10 locos, but at least I copped 8F 48365. Edge Hill held 38, with 'Black Five' 45298 a cop. It was then home for 21.15. Despite the lack of cops, on no day did I see less than two hundred steam locomotives, and this was within two years of steam vanishing from the national network. Tuesday August 23rd was to be the last day of my travels, and I chose Carlisle as my destination. I passed the two J27s being hauled by a class 37 near Howden to their inevitable fate. Once again, 77000 was busy shunting in the Leeds area, and Q6 63387 was seen heading east past Neville Hill with a freight. Upperby shed only held 17 engines, but seven were Britannias. Kingmoor depot was always a delight, but seemed fairly empty with 52 locomotives scattered around the site, including twelve Britannias. I then trundled out to Workington, which was home to just 11 steam engines. Carlisle Upperby was visited again at 18.00, but despite all my efforts that day, I copped absolutely nothing, which was a first for me. However, it had been a great week, with thirty more locomotives underlined in my abc combined volume.

Looking at my diary for the year I seem to constantly mention friends who swore that they'd be going on trips with me, but of course they rarely did. They're now just names scribbled across the page, for only my close companions Mike and Ian could be relied on, with Brian occasionally accompanying me. Anyway, at the time The Who were singing 'I'm a boy', and I had no doubts about it, for I was always ready for one more adventure. I was due to go to the Southern Region on Saturday August 27th, but for some reason the tickets needed weren't available on a bank holiday weekend. That didn't stop me from zooming off to Crewe and Chester instead. Once again the 06.50 to Leeds was my chosen mode of transport, and Jubilees 45562 and 45647 were still hard at work, being spotted at Neville Hill, while sister loco 45565 shunted Central station. I observed fifty locos on the way to Chester, where the depot held 33 engines, including pannier tank 1628 and one of the last 'Crabs', 42782, but I copped nothing. Jubilee 45647 had followed me from Leeds at the head of a Llandudno special. I did better at my old favourite, Croes Newydd, for I copped two here, 75071 and 92105, among the 20 on shed. It was then off to Shrewsbury, where I copped 45311. The shed was home to 39 steam engines, but the G.W.R. influence had now gone completely. I finally visited Crewe South, which held no less than 83 locos. Any serious spotter in the 1960s could go practically blindfolded to the shed, for you went left out the station, and then left down Gresty Lane. You continued down the road until just before the railway overbridge that always advertised 'Mornflakes', and then there was a clearly defined path off to the left. I managed to cop 'Jinty' 47658 while passing Crewe Works, and 9Fs 92013 and 92218 on the shed, which cleared the class for me. It was a terrific day out, but something must have gone wrong, for I was still at Crewe at 20.00, and I didn't get home until after midnight, in the knowledge that I'd copped just six numbers. However, it was all about the thrill of the chase, and I never did things by halves. With The Small Faces, who made number one in the pop charts in September, I could say it was 'All or Nothing' with me.

Chapter 18

I want to tell you

I was always obsessed with ideas to get more money to fund the trips that I envisaged, and in the summer of 1966 it seemed to take the form of playing one armed bandits. I even tried to build one, to con money out of my mates! I'm sure that I put more money into them than I got out, but it didn't stop me trying, especially if my dad gave me some small change when we visited Hornsea by car. However, on Thursday September 1st my dad did better than that, for he drove me to the Cromford and High Peak Railway, a destination which would have been impossible by train. Unfortunately the weather was patchy, and that tended to keep mam and dad in the car rather than enjoy the beautiful Derbyshire Peak District, as I scrambled around these remote depots. Cromford was home to 0F 47006, which was a cop for me, but it was in store, as D2380 had taken over its duties. J94 68012 was still in steam at Middleton, but it was not a cop. However, I was fascinated by the antique ex Midland 0-6-0 acting as a stationary boiler. It was numbered 899, but what that meant in reality, heaven only knows. On the way home, the rain had stopped, and as we drove straight past the scrapyard at Chesterfield, I cajoled my dad to stop, and so I ran down the road to note down B1s 61003, 61061 and 61285 and WD 90315. I was further rewarded by a very much in steam Wakefield WD 90651 storming past on a south bound freight.

At the beginning of September, the Great Central shut as a through route. It had been a special treasure in 1966, for it brought steam traction into London from the north. Motive power was usually provided by Colwick or Banbury, and Britannias still made occasional forays into the capital. Willesden had shut in September 1965, and so that had finished Euston off, and the demise of Western steam had killed off Southall at the turn of the year. The closure of the G.C. also radically reduced the numbers of steam locos that wandered down south to places like Oxford, Reading and even Southern Region metals. I vividly recall seeing an amazing picture of one of Holbeck's Jubilees reaching Bournemouth that summer! Meanwhile up north, the A4s ran their last 3 hour trips on the Glasgow to Aberdeen service. The curtain had finally fallen on their indian summer of express work north of the border. The very last of the glory days for L.N.E.R traction had now come to an end.

The missed Newcastle trip in August had repercussions, for the new issue of 'The Railway Magazine' recorded that the Q6s I needed had just been withdrawn. There was no time to waste, and a trip to the North East was arranged for the following Saturday, September 3rd. Dairycoates scrap line was stacked with withdrawn WDs as I passed on the way to York via Selby. Fortunately, I was in time, for 63435 and 63446 were still on the depot. Additionally, I copped sister engine 63394. I then travelled north to Heaton. Amazingly, the shed was home to two J72s, numbers 58 and 59, plus three K1s, WD 90200, recently transferred from Wakefield to Sunderland, two Q6s, 'Coffee Pot' 43133, and no less than six J27s. Not bad for a shed that closed to steam in 1963! It was then off to Blyth, with 26 locos on the North depot. 'Coffee Pot' and K1 2-6-0s were now starting to push out the ex N.E.R veterans. I copped two of the K1s, 62025 and 62050. Bolckow's scrapyard held four Q6s, J27 65825 and 9F 92062, redundant from the Tyne Dock iron ore workings. The mogul invaders were also infiltrating the South shed, as four 'Coffee Pots' slumbered among the dozen J27s there. By way of change, I bashed Holbeck MPD on my way back home. There were only two Jubilees on shed, numbers 45675 and 45694, rubbing shoulders with an ex N.E.R. intruder, Q6 63387.

The re-arranged Southern trip took place on Friday September 9th, when I boarded the 21.27 train to Doncaster. This outing was to be a first for two reasons. Firstly, even though I'd travelled all over, and been on holiday by myself, I'd never done an overnight jaunt on my own. This was all to change, for I did no fewer than five overnighters in the next seven months, all but one to the Southern Region. Secondly, there were very few steam depots that were virgin territory for me by this late stage, and Weymouth was one of them. That was all to change on the Saturday. I shambled out of Kings Cross at 03.00 and proceeded to walk briskly down Euston Road. The capital was strangely quiet as I glanced down mews and lanes, half expecting to hear the wild parties mentioned in the press whenever 'Swinging London' was in the news. It seems incredible that a fourteen year old should be wandering around London in the small hours, but I rarely met anybody, and I certainly didn't come to any harm. West Country 34015 'Exmouth' was at the head of the 05.30 departure, which was to take me to Eastleigh, and it was a cop for me. Passing Basingstoke I noticed four steamers in for servicing, and the whole day was to be very steamy, with Standard locomotives probably being slightly more numerous than ex Southern types by this time. 70D held thirty five locos, and four were cops to me. Engines from the London Midland Region had now ceased to go to the works for overhaul, and so there were no surprises from that quarter. Standard 2-6-0 76011 was to be my motive power for the 08.38 to Bournemouth, passing a dozen more steamers on the way. I copped a further four more numbers on 70F, out of the 23 engines on shed. In glorious sunshine, Standard 4-6-0 73115, on the 10.49 departure, hauled me through Dorset and towards my prize of the day, Weymouth, 70G.

As a serial shed basher, I always carried an Ian Allan Shed Directory, which gave anyone who bothered to read it the directions to every British depot. It was an essential tool for the job, but it expressly forbade the reader from entering any railway premise without permission. Wise words, but as always, it was wisdom wasted on the young, especially when the young were desperate for those last cops! A brisk walk brought me to the Weymouth MPD, home to 17 steamers. I copped two Ivatt 2-6-2 tanks, 41301 and 41320, but a much needed resident, sister loco 41324, had been sent for scrap, and so eluded my grasp. I also gained Standard 2-6-0 76033. I'd allowed a generous hour and a half to bash the shed, and so there was plenty of time to enjoy the late summer sunshine and saunter back to the station. Here, Battle of Britain pacific 34060 '25 Squadron' was waiting to haul me all the way back to Waterloo. It wasn't a cop, but what a fabulous journey it gave me. With my head out of the window, I sang 'Winchester Cathedral' as I passed the famous town. The New Vaudeville Band had made it to the Top Ten with the track only that week, and so it seemed appropriate! I recorded thirty steam locomotives on my passage back to the Capital, but I wasn't finished yet. No visit to London in 1966 was complete without paying one's respects to the last steam depot in town, Nine Elms, 70A. This decaying cathedral of steam was home to thirty five of the beasts, and I managed to cop two pacifics, 34001 and 34017, and a Standard tank, number 80095. I left Kings Cross station at 18.48, and as the class 47 diesel, the number of which I had absolutely no interest in, hurried me homeward with the sun setting, I looked back on a very successful outing, as I underlined twenty one numbers in my Locoshed book. Not only that, but all haulage on the Southern Region had been courtesy of steam traction. What a day!

The next day, I went to Hornsea and lost more money, dad's fortunately, on one armed bandits. This was a departure from most Sundays, when I'd make the obligatory walk to Dairycoates depot in the afternoon, noting any new arrivals on 'Death Row'. When I arrived back from the coast, I dropped in on Mike, who lived at Cholmley Street Post Office. This was a regular Sabbath occurrence, and as usual I was escorted into a large upstairs room, where Mike was invariably editing some cine film he had taken, or carefully transcribing numbers from a previous day's trip into a permanent logbook. The conversation would follow well worn tracks, such as 'where was the next outing to? or 'what's been withdrawn?', usually followed by a post mortem of recent shed bashing jaunts. This day was different, for Mike, taking the words from a Beatles song on the Revolver album, said there's something 'I want to tell you'. That something was that he'd bought a car. I immediately had pictures of the new Ford Cortina that we'd hired in April for the Lancashire trip. The reality was to be very different, for it was a 1954 Austin Somerset convertible that had seen better days, and a long time in the past too. There was a hole in the floor on the passenger's side, that is on my side, the size of a fist, covered discretely by a piece of carpet. The canvas roof was very draughty and leaked, and the brakes were practically non-existent. How it got through an M.O.T. test I'll never know. To cap it all, it used a pint of oil every fifty miles! So this was to be the chariot of salvation in the coming months, taking us to our Shangri-la, the remaining steam depots!

The following Sunday, September 18th was to be our steed's first try out, with a hop, or rather a rattle, across to the West Riding. I didn't expect too much in the way of cops, and I was correct, only gaining two numbers, 48432 and 90645 on the last depot of the day, Royston. How did our mode of transport perform? Well, we left St. Matthew Street (what, carriage arranged direct from your door, what next!) and started our shed bash at York, always a favourite, and home to 31 locos. There were still a number of B1 and K1s on shed, along with A4 60019 'Bittern', but the J27s were down to just two, 65823 and 65894. Only two V2s remained, numbers 60806 and long time resident 60831, which was to be the last V2, withdrawn in January 1967. In quick succession we romped around Stourton, with 26 on shed, Farnley, then at the point of closure, with 18 on, including Jubilee 45647 'Sturdee' and on to Bradford Manningham, with just 12 locos present, mostly 'Coffee Pots' or Stanier 2-6-4 tanks. Heading south, we raced around Low Moor, home to 15 steamers, including Jubilee 45565 'Victoria', and on to Huddersfield, which was due to close at any time. As to be expected, there were only ten locos there, mostly WDs. Mirfield had a few more months to go, and the tally of twenty steamers, including Britannia 70021, proved more promising and got us in the mood for the depot of the day - Wakefield! No less than 59 engines graced its environs, with 31 being WDs. There was a small sprinkling of B1s, 8Fs and Stanier tanks, but the real treasure was Jubilee 45694 'Bellerophon'. To our chagrin we were thrown out of Normanton MPD, after only being able to record three locos, 61035 'Pronghorn', 48143 and 48160. How could the foreman do it to us, the elite of the trainspotter's art, and on a Sunday too! So with tails between our legs we slunk off to Royston shed, home to 29 steamers, and headed east towards Hull. The cost - ten shillings! Cheap, but chilly, for it was a wet day. We paid our final respects of the day to the giants of steam at Dairycoates. There were 39 locos on shed, of which 14 were for scrap. J27s 65809 and 65811 were being repaired for some reason, prior to being ritually disembowelled at Draper's yard. The ultimate A1, 60145 'Saint Mungo' still clung to life, in the company of fellow express locomotive, Jubilee 45660 'Rooke' and the last Fowler 2-6-4 tank 42394. We'd managed to see over 250 steam engines that day, and all within sixty miles of Hull. It was then home and dreams of greater things, for Mike had a special trip up his sleeve - Wales. At the time I had a plan for a Mid-Wales excursion on the drawing board, to bash the remote depot at Machynlleth. It was to be an overnighter, using a remarkable train, the 21.50 York to Shrewsbury, arriving at the ungodly hour of 03.21. Now that's what I call a class through train for an overnight kip! Furthermore, even at this late date, it was still steam hauled throughout - beat that for a fab outing! However, Mike's motorised plans for the following weekend put paid to this epic journey, and I was destined never to attempt it in real life.

The time was 21.30 as I peered anxiously at my watch under the dim lights of Earlestown station. The date was Friday September

23rd, and I'd left Hull on the 17.53 to Liverpool, hoping to rendezvous with Mike there. Thoughts of 'Homeward Bound' drifted around my head, for Paul Simon is supposed to have got the idea for the song while waiting in that very place. What if Mike didn't show? What if the car had broken down? No mobile phones in those days. Mike had had the day off work and had travelled over earlier for some reason, now lost in the mists of time. Fortunately, he did arrive, and it was off to digs in town for the night. Saturday started with Warrington Dallam depot 8B, home to 21 locos, before heading south west to Shrewsbury 6D. The scene here was more promising than the last time, for there were 38 steamers at home, mostly Standards or 'Black Fives'. Great Western survivor, pannier 8718, a former Stourbridge resident, was obviously on its way to the great train set in the sky, but it was a welcome sight anyway on its old stomping ground. We then zoomed into Central Wales, destination Machynlleth, 6F. Again, this was virgin territory for me, and I copped 46521 and 75009 among the five locos on shed. Mike and I watched as a Talyllyn excursion, double headed by Standard 4-6-0s 75002 and 75029 called at the location. It was then off to Porthmadog, or somewhere similar, for Mike was an observer member of the Association of Railway Preservation Societies, and they were holding a meeting there. I stayed in the car and was bored out of my skull. Not a single steam engine passed, and I was glad to get to the digs in Bangor and crash out.

Sunday promised better things for it was sunny as we trundled up to Holyhead, which was home to just eight locos, all but 'Jinty' 47410 and Standard 4-6-0 73006 being 'Black Fives'. Nine steamers slumbered on Llandudno Junction, but none were cops for me. The shed was to shut to steam a fortnight later. Birkenhead beckoned, '9F city', with 21 of the beasts among the 44 engines present. Five 'Crabs' hung on there, along with four Jinties, and a visitor from, yes, you guessed it, Wakefield, in the guise of WD 90409. Chester held even more locomotives, 46 in total, and I even copped one, 45132. There were no less than six Jinties clinging to life in the border town, and 'Crab' 42942 was visiting from Birkenhead. We then headed back towards Wales with a dash around Croes Newydd. Of the 24 engines resting there, two were cops, 75033 and 75052. The old order died hard in Wrexham, and panniers 1628, 1638, 3709, 8767 and 9641 were to be among the final Great Western engines to be withdrawn, all by the end of

1966. We then headed homeward, and nestling among 15 other locos on Northwich shed were two cops, 48640 and 48683. The car had behaved impeccably, that is, I was still alive, and the oil consumption had been a consistent 50 miles to the pint. The weekend had cost me 65/9 (doesn't the old currency look more impressive!), and I'd copped 11 numbers. The future looked automobile powered, for Mike had obviously taken note of The Beatles track 'Drive my car'!

Chapter 19

Friday on my mind

I'd been promoted from the B stream up to 4A in September 1966, and even though I worked hard at my studies at Riley High School, like the Easybeats, who charted the following month, I always had 'Friday on my mind'. That is, the weekend called, and the next train trip. My diary notes that by this time, I only needed 71 steam engines that were, as far as I knew, still in capital stock. A few would come to me, or rather Draper's scrapyard upon the Grim Reaper's beckoning, but the rest were located as far apart as Bournemouth in Dorset and Thornton Junction in Fife! Just after the cryptic note of 45581 'Bihar and Orissa', 42110, 48264, 92098, 92164, 92217 and 92247 arriving for scrap on October 1st, there is the authoritative entry on October 6th that 'Hull may be steam for the next 4 years!' That was a big may, but it was typical of the rumours of the day. 1970 had long been bandied about as being the year that would see the demise of my beloved steam locomotives, but it proved to be woefully wrong. The Hollies charted in October with 'Stop, stop, stop', and that's what I wanted British Railways to do with the dismantling of steam locomotives, but it wasn't to be. The month brought foreigners, 4Fs 44311 and 44500, screeching and squealing all the way from Barrow to satisfy Drapers lust for scrap, but it also brought Hull Fair - and one armed bandits! By now, you're probably fearing the worst, and you'd be right to do so, for looking at my diary, I'd obviously dropped many a copper into their rapacious maw. However, on Saturday 8th, I found a faulty thruppenny bit machine, and milked it for all it was worth. When I noticed the attendants starting to eye me up suspiciously, I beat a hasty retreat, but not before I was thirty four shillings better off! That was a fortune in those days. To put this in context, I had just had a pocket money increase from five to seven shillings, so that sum represented nearly five weeks income! However, karma is always around the corner to catch you out, for I'd taken my bike and left it in a dark corner of West Park. No, it hadn't been stolen, but I had locked it and forgotten to bring the key! So with a pocket bulging with shiny coins, I had to carry my bike over Anlaby Road flyover and down the Boulevard. It was a good job that no policemen spotted me, or I might have had some explaining to do.

The funds were to come in handy, for my next foray was to be over the border on Friday 21st, leaving Hull Paragon at 21.31 for York. This was my second overnighter, and my only one to Scotland. My July jaunt up north had not cleared my Scottish tally, for three numbers were still needed, and it was very late days indeed for Scottish steam. The final A4s had gone the previous month, and by the year's end there were to be only 62 steam engines in capital stock north of the border. Not that steam disappeared quickly in Scotland. Far from it, for the former G.N.O.S.R. lines had been dieselised as long ago as 1961. It was then a war of slow attrition, as the allocations of the surviving sheds gradually dwindled away, until, by June 1967, they'd vanished altogether. Twenty six locos were on York depot, with the brace of V2s, 60806 and 60831, just hanging on, but the J27s had gone. Merchant Navy 35026 'Lamport & Holt Line' was obviously on a special up north, and 'Black Five' 45363 was a long way from its home at Carlisle Kingmoor. I left York just before midnight, arriving in Edinburgh Waverley at the ungodly hour of 03.26. My train to Fife wasn't until 06.10, and I spent a very cold two and a half hours in one of the phone booths on the concourse. That was the price of commitment to the chase. Well. I certainly should have been committed! Thornton Junction was my first destination, and in the weak autumn sun, I crunched up the cinder path and into the depot at 07.30. The shed was busy, for it was home to 31 steamers, which at this eleventh hour was probably a record for a Scottish steam depot. J36 65327 was still the stationary boiler, but it had regal company, in the form of A4 60009 'Union of South Africa', which was waiting to enter preservation at nearby Markinch. But what mattered to me was the kill, and it was there, J38 65914! With one down, and two to go, it was off to Glasgow, and Corkerhill. 67A was home to thirty engines, and once again I was lucky, for Standard 2-6-0 76093 was lurking in its midst. It was then a short hop out to Motherwell, 66B, which was surprisingly full, with 25 steamers present. Five were 'Crabs' from Ayr, and as that depot shut to steam the same month, I now have to assume that they were heading for a local breaker. Not that I knew that at the time - no instant communications then! However, no cops were forthcoming, and so I hoped for better things from Carstairs Junction, 66E. This windy spot was home to just 17 locos, but at least I scored another bullseye with Stanier tank, 42058.

Something must have gone awry that day, for my plotted timetable has the ominous words 'Times changed' struck through them. Having cleared my Scottish tally, my desire was now to travel the full length of the Waverley Route in daytime, but to do this I needed to get back to Edinburgh. It was taking a bit of a liberty with my weekend return to Glasgow, but these were desperate times, and so desperate measures were needed. This is when disaster struck, for the next train to Edinburgh was cancelled, and there weren't that many of them anyway. What to do? My saviour appeared in the guise of a Scottish lady in a similar dilemma, who politely asked 'Do you want to share my taxi? I've just booked one.' No guessing my reply! At Waverley station, after thanking my benefactor for the favour for which she would take no payment, I enquired about the next departure on the Waverley Route. When it arrived, I snuggled down into the welcoming embrace of its steam heating, for it was my first chance to warm myself since the overnight journey up the East Coast. I noted J36 65234 still supplying steam at St. Margarets MPD as I passed the depot at 15.04, and then settled down for the vista that I was sure was to unfold as the train climbed the Cheviot Hills. Next thing I knew I was in Carlisle! Tiredness and steam heating had done the trick, and I was never destined to travel this beautiful route again, for it closed in 1969, despite much local protestation. I just had time for Carlisle Upperby shed, as I never, ever, wasted an opportunity to bash another shed. There were 27 steamers, seven of them Britannias, visible in the rapidly gathering gloom, before I ran down Botchergate to catch the last train that I could, at about 18.45, to arrive home at 22.46. Originally, I had intended the trip to be a double overnighter, for I had planned to bash several more Scottish depots, before leaving Glasgow Queen Street at 21.25, but as I've already commented, something went horribly adrift that day, and I now have no recollection of what that something was.

My next jaunt was to be in the Mikemobile, registration ODT 709, on November 5th. The destination was Geordie Land, and I was deadweight once again i.e. there to fund the petrol, and also to cop just one engine - K1 62023, and so clear all my North Eastern numbers. West Hartlepool was our first venue. There were only eleven on shed, but no less than four freights passed as we romped around the site. Sunderland was home to fourteen engines, and Tyne Dock to 17. Even travelling by car we noted several steam hauled local freights. Obviously all the numbers seen were standard North Eastern fare, with a few WDs and the 9Fs for the Consett iron ore trains. 62023 had been transferred down from Tweedmouth when the depot shut in June, but it was not on 52H. Panic ensued, Mike wanted to press on, and I wanted to stay a little longer. The day was saved when, at 14.15, the K1 trundled into sight heading for the ramshackle shed that it called home, albeit for only a few months more. It was then across the Tyne to bash the two Blyth depots in failing light. Thirteen engines were on the South shed and 27 on the North, but only three J27s remained, now eclipsed by K1s, B1s and 'Coffee Pots' redundant from elsewhere. Bolckow's yard was ready to devour 62022, 63363, 63406, 63454, 65790, 65801, 65802 and 65859. It was then homeward, with just one cop, and my pocket 19/6 the lighter.

With Banbury closing to steam in October, there were now only two surviving steam depots that were virgin territory for me, and one was Barrow in Furness. Little did I realise how fine I was cutting it when I visited the depot on November 26th, for it was to close to steam the following month. The vestibule anthem for the day was The Beach Boys classic 'Good Vibrations', which was riding high in the charts at the time. I noted little on the way to Carnforth, but the tally of fifty seven on shed was good. The day was very dark and wet, and I felt anything but good vibrations as I walked the mile down Rawlinson Street to the shed. The run down nature of the location added to the general gloom, but I managed to cop three inhabitants, 45141, 47373 and 47675, among the 14 locos present. My spirits lifted when I discovered that Britannia 70053 'Moray Firth', the loco that had hauled me there on the 11.29 from Carnforth, was to haul the 13.46 Euston train. I alighted at Carnforth and after doing the shed again, I settled down to watch the world, and steam engines, pass by until my train at 17.02. The lights of Shipley station illuminated Britannia 70006 'Robert Burns' on a west bound passenger train, but otherwise little was seen on my journey home, with just three cops, the same as the Scottish bash, but for rather less money.

As November turned to December, Stanier 'Crab' 42963 had joined 45581 'Bihar and Orissa' on the scrapline, and kept 45207, 61012, 'Puku' (an old Hull favourite), 61032 'Stembok', 63409, 63453, 65809 and 90652 company. Even at this late date, there were still quite a variety of locomotives being broken up by Albert Draper. I also took up stamp collecting, United Kingdom only, but that fad didn't last long, for it hardly had the thrill of the chase. Incidentally, I have never been hooked on T.V., but I do recall several series then that I did stay in to watch. They were 'The Man from U.N.C.L.E.', 'Get Smart', the spoof spy programme, and the cult thriller 'Adam Adamant' with Gerald Harper. Last, but not least, was 'Vendetta', which was broadcast on a Friday night. On December 16th I watched an episode and then trudged down to Paragon Station to catch the 21.27 to Doncaster, for I was off to London, and was due to revisit the Southern Region the following day. My initial port of call was to be Basingstoke. The stabling point held nine locos, four Bulleid pacifics and five Standard types. Ominously, I noted D1923 at Waterloo at the head of the 05.30 Southampton train as I headed westward. Trudging over the Campbell Road railway bridge towards Eastleigh shed, I noticed preserved 34051 'Winston Churchill' waiting to greet me in the Eastleigh works yard. The main depot held just twenty five engines, but at least I copped U.S.A tank 30071 and Standard 76059. The Isle of Wight now beckoned, for steam operation was due to finish there on the last day of 1966. O2s 14, 16, 17 (which I copped), 20, 24, 33 and 35 were on Ryde shed. I then took time to travel out to Shanklin behind number 24. I copped No. 27 at Ryde Esplanade station, and fellow locomotive, No.31 near Sandown. It was a sunny day, and my last memories of this magic isle are of No. 20 banking our train, hauled by No. 28, from Ryde St. Johns to Ryde Esplanade. It was then back to the mainland, and a quick bash of Fratton stabling point. Amazingly, I copped Standard 2-6-0 76031, which along with 2-6-4T 80139, were the only two steamers on the shed. There was still time for one last shed, Guildford, and in the failing light, I strode around the semi-roundhouse, carefully noting down the 14 engines sheltering there, of which two were Bulleid pacifics, 34012 and 35008. It was dark by the time I recorded 34036 at Waterloo and I was then subsumed into the chaos that was, and is, the rush hour on the London Underground. As I rattled north on the 18.20 departure from Kings Cross, I considered that I had done well, for I'd copped six. However, I still hadn't cleared my tally of Southern steam, and time was fast running out. It was the deepest and darkest depths of winter, and for steam there was no light at the end of the tunnel. Indeed, The Move song 'Night of fear' seemed to encapsulate the mood of impending doom perfectly.

Chapter 20

I'm a believer

Christmas 1966 was the time that those manufactured pop interlopers from America, The Monkees, exploded onto the U.K. music scene. Yes, 'I'm a believer' in steam traction, but 'The last train to Clarksville' was unlikely to be steam powered by this time. While they were conquering the pop charts, I was planning my next excursion, for my father's ship was berthed at Newport, and he was prepared to pay for me to visit him. Despite a week of illness at Christmas, over my fifteenth birthday, I set off on December 29th to South Wales to meet him, with one or two diversions on the way. Leaving Hull on the 06.13, in the first light of dawn I made out the shapes of 41528, 41708, 41734, 41763, 41804, 41835 and 47005 stored outside Rotherham Masborough station. My destination was Toton depot, facilitated by a bus ride from Derby. I regularly updated my Locoshed book, courtesy of 'The Railway Magazine', but for some inexplicable reason, I still had Standard 2-6-0s numbers 78044 and 78055 allocated to the shed, and I needed them. Actually, the depot had been completely dieselised from December 1965, but facts like that were often overlooked in the world of rapid change that was the 1960s railway scene. Anyway, there were two 2-6-0s on shed, numbers 78061 and 78064, but I didn't need this pair of beauties! Unbeknown to me, 78044 and 78055 had been transferred to Bolton. I caught up with the first, but not the second engine, and so it eluded my grasp and was devoured, unseen, by the breaker's relentless maw. Derby still had some steam activity, and I noted 0F 47000 on shed. However, Burton depot had shut to steam two months previously and was home to a dejected 8F 48286, in appalling condition. Ominously, my log book has no entries of any steam activity between Derby and my next port of call, Birmingham.

My worst fears were confirmed as I strode around Tyseley MPD. There were fifteen locos on shed, but all were dead. The old order, in suspended animation, hung on in the familiar numbers of 1638, 4176, 4696, 9610, 9630 and 9774. Curiously, I noted that Standards 73127 and 73130 were in the diesel shops, and it was only months later that the trainspotting fraternity realised that Tyseley depot was still undertaking wheel turning for locomotives from further north. I recorded 43026, 44966, 45438, 48747 and 75054 in a scrapyard on the way to Wolverhampton. Oxley was still home to 36 engines, and there I made the only cop of the day, and a very valuable one at that, of G.W.R. pannier tank, number 9658. Additionally, opposite the shed there were 7 locos stored - 1628, 48263, 48274, 48311, 48428, 47631 and 76035. The light was fading fast as I headed back to Birmingham. I then headed south to meet up with my dad at Newport.

The next day I revisited Barry, for locomotives were still being dispatched there. However, I only copped six numbers there, 5051, 6984, 7903, 34092, 35022 and 80072, out of the 178 that I recorded. Remarkably, I have no note of visiting Cashmore's yard at Newport, despite the fact that my father's ship must have been within a mile of this famous steam graveyard. I spent the New Year on board, and then headed home. The sight of Manor 7808 and 0-6-2 tank 6697 at Ashchurch was some small consolation for many miles of steam free territory. The once mighty depot of Saltley was now down to just 16 inhabitants, mostly 9Fs and 'Black Fives'. I copped 8F 48177 as I passed Derby, on my way to Colwick. The former L.N.E.R residents were now long gone, apart from B1, Departmental No.29, and even the population of L.M.S. motive power had been decimated. The shed held thirty steamers. Amazingly, none were Standard types. Records suggest that the depot had shut to steam in December, but I distinctly remember some locos being in steam under the weak January sun. I then turned my back on this wonderful shed for the last time, and headed home, with just eight cops.

Draper's yard was in overdrive as 1966 became 1967, and my diary notes 43020, 43141, 45063, 48127, 48137, 48186, 48196, 48339, 48432, 48443, 48670 and 92075 keeping the former Crewe Works pilots, ex Midland 4Fs 44377 and 44525, company on Dairycoates 7 section. The rumour of the arrival of Paxman diesels was confirmed when a test train passed over the 'top line', that is, the Hull and Barnsley route around the city, and opposite Riley High School, on Thursday January 19th as I looked out from the chemistry lab. Not that I had time to worry about this very unwelcome event, for dad's ship was now berthed in Cardiff dock, and at 07.15 on Saturday 21st, I was off once more, expenses paid, to South Wales. The same sad line of old timers was still awaiting their unenviable fate at Rotherham, with B1, Departmental

No 32 stored nearby. 45464 had joined the derelict 8F at Burton, and therefore it was a great pleasure to note 9F 92166 heading south on a freight at Kings Norton a little while later. The sight of Princess pacific 46201 at Ashchurch, and a cop, was a thrill, but I observed no steamers at all after that, even on Gloucester, Severn Tunnel Junction and Newport Ebbw Junction depots. I took the time to travel to Radyr, and Llantrisant, but they were definitely steam free zones. I had to console myself with the cop of the yard pilot at R.S. Hayes yard at Bridgend, pannier 9642, before meeting my dad at Cardiff.

After spending Sunday on the ship, I travelled back on the Monday. I should have been at school, but expenses paid visits to remote parts seemed much more educational to me! Leaving Cardiff at 08.20, my journey took me via Gloucester and Stratford upon Avon, for I hoped to get a glimpse of engines at the breaker's yard at Long Marston, but in the event the cupboard was bare. It was then on to Wolverhampton, and 'Good day sunshine' to Oxley MPD once more, for it was unseasonably warm. Including the scrapline opposite, there were now 38 locos present, and I copped two, 45308 and 48061. The shed was still home to four panniers, 1628, 3605, 3782 and 9658, but of course, none were in steam. I then headed home, and was to see an amazing, but sombre spectacle, at Derby station at sunset. 8F 48556 pulled in with no fewer than nine 'Jinties' in tow, numbers 47384, 47397, 47482, 47494, 47530, 47615, 47649, 47658, 47661, and additionally, Ivatt 2-6-0 46495. All were Crewe engines, or rather, had been. The 8F, obviously exhausted by its efforts, then retired to the adjacent depot to satisfy its living needs, leaving the dead to their own devices. But the day was not yet over, for a small detour took me to my old favourite, York. In the dark, I trudged around the vast site. A4 60019 'Bittern' was in residence in the roundhouse, along with L.M.S. interlopers 'Black Five' 45005, 8F 48265 and Jubilee 45675 'Hardy'. Long time stalwart V2 60831, having served faithfully, had now been dispatched to a dark corner of the scrapline, along with Q6 63459 and J27 65873. All were awaiting their final call to Hull, and thence oblivion.

The following week my diary records in utter horror the spectacle of no less than seventeen Paxman diesels on Dairycoates depot. I can remember the sight of these misfits gathered around the outside turntable, like some plague of ruthless predators, ready to kill off the last of Hull's steam fleet. Death to the diesels was the cry, but in the event the day was saved by the pathetic braking power of these unloved and unwanted intruders. The Rolling Stones, at number one that week, might have wanted to 'Spend the night together' with one of these monsters, but I wished them in Hell. Initially, they took over most of the local duties, and my beloved WDs and B1s sat disconsolate in the vast roundhouse. However, within days we noticed these pathetic excuses for engines being piloted around Hull's top line by steam locomotives. Apparently, they couldn't stop the loads previously hauled by the steamers in time! It only bought so much time though, for ultimately, when enough of these varmints arrived, the freights were double headed across the city.

Two events occurred in February that were to rock the world. Firstly, The Beatles did not make number one with 'Penny Lane'. Was this the beginning of the end for the Fab Four? Secondly, on Friday 10th, my mother bought me a Tatra classical guitar for sixteen pounds and fifteen shillings from the music department on the top floor of Hammonds store! Brian had got a guitar for Christmas, and I told him that he was mad, but of course, as a teenager, I couldn't be left behind, especially as girls were now entering the equation! Ultimately, that journey up town with my mam to purchase some wood and wire was to have far reaching implications, for music was to become my life, my love, and ultimately my career. Steam couldn't be saved, it was in a terminal decline that would end in August 1968, but life, and the music, had to go on.

Not that I had time to ponder such profound thoughts, for within hours of this significant purchase, I was heading south on a weekend jaunt to the Southern Region. I was determined to hit some of the spots that had eluded me previously, and so I headed to Lancing Works, Redhill and finally Ashford. Apart from two Standard tanks at Waterloo, there was no sign of steam anywhere, apart from preserved O1, 31065, siting forlornly in Ashford shed. I tried to get a peek inside the works for the remaining pilots, two Class Cs and two U.S.A. tanks, but I drew a blank. Heading for safer and steamier climes, I dropped in on Guildford depot. Home to just nine steamers, I managed to cop 73093 before striking out for Basingstoke, with ten residents, but unfortunately no cops. In rapidly failing light, I headed for my ultimate virgin territory, 70E

Salisbury. It was dark as I crept past the foreman's office and into the depot. I just could not risk being thrown out of this prize, and stealth was the name of the game. The depot was home to just a dozen locomotives, but none were cops. Disappointed, I trudged back to the station, but at least it was one more depot underlined as a conquest, the last of many spanning five years. Not that there was time to waste, for I was due to stay at Bournemouth Y.M.C.A. that night, and there was the shed to bash before then. I slunk around 70F and recorded 17 engines under the lights of the shed yard, but again, I drew a blank. Retiring to my digs, I slept well.

The following morning I had a quick breakfast, and after the payment of ten shillings for my night's stay, I left the town on the 08.55 to Eastleigh. The copping of M7 30053, in the company of 34051 'Winston Churchill' in the works yard boded well, and so it was to be, for out of the 26 steamers on shed, I copped no less than four, a record at that late date. They were 30067, 73029, 75074 and 76018. A dash around Basingstoke once more added nine more numbers, before I headed for the capital, and Nine Elms of course. The sun was streaming down as I walked down Brooklands Road and into the shed. There was a hint of spring in the air as I ambled around the ash strewn lines that were home to its 31 inhabitants. I even copped two, 34013 and 76058, before I returned to Waterloo and copped another loco, 80140, on empty coaching stock in the terminus. I headed home with ten cops in the bag, but blissfully unaware that it was the last time that I would ever see Nine Elms depot. The world was indeed changing, for I was not hauled by a single steam locomotive that weekend. Jimi Hendrix was in the throes of redefining the pop universe, first with 'Hey Joe' and then with 'Purple Haze'. The Beatles might well have thought that 'Strawberry Fields' were forever, but as time was to prove, neither they, nor steam traction, had long to go.

Chapter 21

I can hear the grass grow

Initially, I really struggled with learning to play the guitar, for the book that came with it was worse than useless, like so many instruction books. Salvation arrived, if that's the word, in the form of a German language teacher, who started guitar lessons on a Tuesday after school. My first class was on February 28th, and from then on, I never looked back. Of course I still visited Dairycoates depot every day, and recorded the plethora of engines that were now arriving in Hull for scrap. To list them all would be tedious, but in the realms of the living, Standard 2-6-0 77012 was seen on the 'top line' on Wednesday March 8th, in charge of a director's special. Britannia 70025 'Western Star' made a very rare appearance on March 18th at the head of a Barrow in Furness rugby special, for I personally had never seen one of these locomotives in Hull before. I seemed to gain an interest in railway modelling at this time, and I had a TT gauge layout in my bedroom, but it was never to be a serious passion for me, for there was nothing like chasing the real thing. A school trip to Harrogate on Tuesday March 14th came and went, with most of the steam locomotives seen on the day being on Dairycoates scrapline. The final V2, 60831, was among the ranks of the soon to be departed. On March 30th, we had a party for Tony, for he was due to emigrate to Canada the following day. It was Tony who'd driven us down to Peterborough in October 1964. This was a sad loss for the youth club, for he'd been one of its leaders. I'd now started attending the club, which was held in the church hall on the corner of Gordon Street and the Boulevard on a Friday night. I'd also started to grow my hair, in a fringe of course, just like The Beatles, and I figured that being a guitarist was decidedly cool, for I was much more likely to get a girl friend as a musician, than by saying that I was a trainspotter!

You would have thought that my February romp to the Southern had cleared the slate, but that was not the case, and on Friday April 7th, at the usual time of 21.27, I set off for Eastleigh one last time. I managed steam haulage from Waterloo behind Standard 4-6-0 73085 on the 04.40 Woking train. I would normally have caught the 05.30 Southampton departure, but the chance of a steamer was too good to miss. Eastleigh depot was home to 28 locos, but alas, my quest, Standard 2-6-0 76066, was nowhere to be seen. You'll probably think 'You're mad! You went overnight all the way to Eastleigh - for one cop!' Well, you'd be right, for that is what I did. Walking back to the station, unsure what to do, I heard a whistle, and as if by magic, my final Southern cop went past me on an up passenger working. Overjoyed, I boarded a London bound train, with the intention of visiting Neasden, in search of the pannier tanks employed on the London Underground. In the capital, I made the mistake of visiting the old B.R. depot at Neasden, and of course it was empty and dilapidated. The depot I really needed was further down the line towards Queens Park, but I was tired and headed for home. Looking back, that was a valuable opportunity lost, but I was still only fifteen, and so not every decision made sense. I travelled north on a midday Pullman, and to add insult to injury, that cost me extra. I got back to Hull in time to see the second half of the Hull F.C. versus Keighley match. I'd started to take an interest in rugby league, for Mike was a keen supporter of the game.

The Mikemobile was out in force once more on Sunday April 16th, with a drive out to the fledgling Keighley and Worth Valley Railway at Haworth. Ivatt 2-6-2 tank 41241 was in steam at the head of a solitary coach. I noted Royal Scot 46115 ' Scots Guardsman', L.Y.R. No 957, J52 68846, J72 No 59 and N2 65923. We dropped in on Skipton MPD for old time's sake, but it had shut to steam the previous month, and was only home to 47293, 47599 and 75017. On the way back we were treated to the spectacle of 4472 'Flying Scotsman' and 3442 'The Great Marquess' in steam at Leeds Central station.

The railway scene was now moving almost too rapidly to keep pace with. On March 6th, Derby shed shut to steam. To me, it was a miracle that it had stayed open for so long, as it seemed to be heavily dieselised when I first visited the depot in April 1964. Saltley and Oxley had fallen the same day, and so there was now no steam operation left in either the East Midlands, or the West Midlands. Even worse, an old favourite, Shrewsbury, had also gone, and so steam haulage on the Mid-Wales line to Aberystwyth had vanished. At a stroke, with the exception of the Southern Region, which was to hang on for another four months, steam had disappeared south of Stoke on Trent. Despite this capitulation to diesel power, there were still highlights to be seen. One such highlight was the Red Bank (Manchester) to Newcastle parcels. Even in 1967 it was predominantly steam hauled, and was often double headed. I believe it continued to use steam as late as August, being steam hauled throughout, which must have raised a few eyebrows on the East Coast main line north of York.

Hull was not faring well steam-wise, for I noted that on Monday May 8th, all trains on the top line were diesel hauled, although steam did reappear spasmodically after that date. The reality was that most of the remaining steamers in Hull had departed at the beginning of May, leaving about half a dozen to soldier on until June. At this late stage, the coaling plant was abandoned when it ran out of coal, and engines were fuelled by a conveyor belt near the diesel depot. There still was some steam operation, and the sight of double headed WDs seemed to become more common, but the glory days were now well and truly departed. However, even at this late stage, a steamer would often work into Hull to 'pass out' firemen as drivers. The few remaining Jubilees from Leeds Holbeck seemed to be the mainstay for these duties. 'Black Five' 44767 hauling a line of scrap locomotives into Hull on Friday 19th added a spark of interest, but Mike and I now had to look further afield for significant steam activity. To this end, a grand bumper trip to clear all the engines that we now needed was planned for the bank holiday weekend at the end of May.

We set off at 06.00 on Saturday May 27th for Buxton. By this time, I needed just twenty five numbers, and incredibly I notched up two of them on this small depot - 48376 and 68006! There were 14 locos on shed, mostly 8Fs, but four Ivatt 46xxx moguls added a little variety. We dropped in at Peak Forest to watch two 8Fs working the trains at the quarry, and then it was off to Stoke. Thirty six engines later, we were on the road to Crewe. South shed held 58 steamers, and I copped a further two - 44681 and 45292. Three Britannias, 70005, 70031 and 70045 graced the depot, but pride of place went to 71000 'Duke of Gloucester'. Despite the January clear out, a solitary 'Jinty', 47566, hid in the shed's depths, perhaps hoping to escape the notice of the authorities. Croes Newydd held 17 steamers, nearly all being Standard types. Motive power wise there was now no sign of its Great Western origins. Chester's tally of 34 added another cop to my list - 48287, and Northwich's 25 inhabitants yielded 45065. This was don't stop until you drop trainspotting, pure 'the more you dash, the more you bash' adrenaline rush! We didn't have time to watch the grass grow, let alone time to sing with The Move 'I can hear the grass grow'! Warrington Dallam was home to 18, but no cops, and we even dropped in on Warrington Central station to find 44866, 48349 and 48356 stabled there. Sutton Oak next, with 17 engines, was followed by Aintree. I scored again here, with 44910 among the 15 locos on shed, before the Mikemobile crossed the Mersey. Birkenhead was home to 45 steamers. WDs 90362 and 90650 were a long way from their home at Normanton. No less than 34 9Fs were on shed, so the sight of 'Crab' 42942 and a few Stanier tanks made a welcome change. With our digs for the night located at Newton-le-Willows, we travelled back across the river and zoomed into Edge Hill. The depot was packed, with no less than 54 locos scattered around the sprawling site. The 'Jinties' had gone, and most of the tally were 'Black Fives', 8Fs and 9Fs. The last call of the day was Speke Junction, and here I copped 45263 among its 35 residents. So I was off to our B&B with all of nine cops under my belt on the first day of our grand Northern shed bash! We'd done twelve sheds and one stabling point, and seen nearly 380 steam locomotives within the space of twelve hours. Glorious days indeed!

The next day we romped around Springs Branch, home to 55 locos, including the last Stanier 'Crab', 42954, and one cop for me - 44920. Bolton was next, with 45 on, and two cops, 48384, and the Standard that had eluded me at Toton, 78044. No less than 57 steamers were stabled on Patricroft, and I copped 45092. Britannias were getting everywhere in those days, and Patricroft was no exception, for a brace of them, 70027 'Rising Star' and 70033 'Charles Dickens' were on shed. I copped diminutive 'Lanky Pug' 51218 at Trafford Park, along with more mundane 'Black Five' 44965. The shed was home to 43 locos, including a number of Stanier 2-6-4 tanks. For some reason that now escapes me, we then backtracked to Stoke. I suspect Mike needed something from there, for we dashed around the depot missing out the scrapline altogether, and then headed off for Heaton Mersey depot. As it was a Sunday, no less than 40 steamers were on shed, and I copped 48637, but all the Stanier 'Crabs' had now gone. Even the glimpse of a 'Jinty' was of interest by the summer of 1967, such was the lack of variety on the steam scene. Jubilee 45596 'Bahamas' was still at home on Stockport Edgeley, along with 31 other residents, including 48170, a cop for me. It was then off to Manchester, and Newton Heath, naturally. There were 64 engines there, including one more for the road - 48620. It was about this time that two or three antique Lancashire and Yorkshire Railway 0-6-0s appeared at the shed. They'd been steam heating boilers nearby, and seemed to surface after being withdrawn thirty years! It all added to the magic and mystery that were the final years of steam, and showed that surprises could still turn up. Not that we had time to ponder this, for we were then venturing into deepest East Lancashire. As I've already commented, Mike's car was less than roadworthy, particularly in the brake department. I clearly remember freewheeling down a steep hill into Burnley, with the engine turned off, to save fuel! Foolhardy in the extreme, and yet I've survived to tell the tale. Rose Grove was home to 25 engines, and most importantly to me, 'Black Five' 45275. 52 locomotives graced Lostock Hall, the last shed of the day. I copped 78020, and we even saw a 'Jinty' - 47326! Ten depots in a day, if you include our short interlude at Stoke, and we'd seen no less than 400 steam locomotives.

Sunday had been sunny, but Monday was to be even warmer, as we left our digs at Lancaster and descended on Carnforth shed. Home to 56 steamers, I copped none, but it was a pleasure to see the preserved L.T.S.R. tank 'Thundersley' on display. Tebay held seven Standard 4-6-0s and a solitary Stanier 2-6-4 tank, 42134, all for banking duties on Shap. By this time, Carlisle Upperby was shut to steam, but you would never have guessed it from a walk round the place. Twenty four steam locomotives were stabled there, including four Britannias and four Ivatt 46xxxx 2-6-0s. The biggest surprise of the day was Kingmoor depot, for it was home to no less than 106 steam engines! That was the greatest tally that I personally ever saw on a depot, not having been old enough to savour the delights of Stratford in the 1950s. I copped just one, 'Black Five' 44672, but also present were 'Jinties' 47471 and 47641 and no less than 23 Britannias! It was then off to the East Coast, and Heaton depot. Eleven locos, including J72 No 58, B1 61238 'Leslie Runciman', and several 'Coffee Pots' and K1s were present. Sunderland held 27 engines, mostly J27s, but nine WDs had intruded on this North Eastern stronghold. The last shed of the day was West Hartlepool, with only two Q6s among the 21 steamers present. Again, WDs were starting to outnumber the old order, for there were 12 of them on shed. It was then off to

Mike's uncle's in Darlington for a night's rest, having seen another 250 engines.

The last day of our 'Magical Mystery Tour' was a pure delight, for Mike wanted to visit the colliery lines of County Durham. We spent time at Ryhope Junction watching Q6s going about the duties that they had performed for decades, before visiting the Seaham Harbour Railway, the South Hetton branch, and the grand prize of them all - the Philadelphia Railway. The depot alone held 18 engines, including former Taff Vale Railway tank, G.W.R. No 426. In glorious sunshine, we strolled around this industrial site, just enjoying the moment. Too soon, it was time to travel home, but we could always find time for one last shed visit - York. How had the mighty fallen, for it was home to just 13 locos, with only five in steam, Jubilee 45562 'Alberta' from Holbeck, B1s 61012 'Puku', an old Hull favourite, 61021 'Reitbok', 61237 'Geoffrey H. Kitson', and finally, Standard 2-6-0 77012. A hint of former glories was present in the shape of two A4s, 4498 'Sir Nigel Gresley' and 60019 'Bittern'. We arrived home on the evening of Tuesday May 30th after four days, having covered 916 miles, and having seen well over one thousand steam locomotives. Even now, with the benefit of hindsight and the knowledge that steam was to vanish within fifteen months, this trip was a trainspotting piece de resistance. It was almost like my final curtain call, before I watched the closing scenes, and the enfolding tragedy of the last days of steam from the wings.

Chapter 22

A day in the life (of a shed basher)

On June 1st, The Beatles released 'Sgt. Pepper's Lonely Hearts Club Band', and pop music entered a new phase of its existence. Like John, Paul, George and Ringo, I was 'Getting Better' on the guitar, but things were definitely not getting better on the steam front. The sight of WD 90695 on June 8th was my last record of regular steam operation around Hull. I'd got a Brownie camera and I took a few shots of the last days of steam at Dairycoates, but the results were pretty dismal. On Saturday June 17th, Mike and I drove out to Selby to see 4472 'Flying Scotsman' on a north bound excursion. Steam was now getting so scarce that I even took a photograph of a steam crane on the riverside at the B.O.C.M. mill! We dropped in at Goole, which was home to thirty engines, but all were dead. There were four B1s, with the rest being WDs, including 90695. The shed had abandoned steam on June 12th. I've read other dates for the dieselisation of Hull, Goole and York, but June 12th looks right to me. York held just eleven locomotives, all in store, plus visitor 60019 'Bittern'. From there we travelled to a steam rally at Castle Howard. It was a brilliantly sunny day, and Mike took the hood down on his convertible Austin Somerset. I've never understood the passion for this style of travel, for we may have looked really cool, but I certainly felt cool, even on this hot day! Into the bargain, I arrived home with a splitting headache. Our trip out that day demonstrated to Mike and I that we now had to look to the West Riding for active steam.

On June 24th, we went on our grand 'End of West Riding Steam Tour', starting at Normanton MPD. There were 32 locos on shed, and most were in steam, for the depot was to become the last servicing facility for steam on the North Eastern Region, finally finishing on January 1st 1968. Most were WDs, but Standard 73045 was visiting from Patricroft. Stanier tanks 42085, 42093 and 42138 were the first of a number that we saw that day, and were still doing sterling work in the area. Our second depot was to be the biggest shock of the day. Wakefield had always been the jewel among the West Riding sheds, but that day it appeared more like the 'Marie Celeste' of train operation. It was like a ghost town, for there was no one in sight, and all the offices had been left open and their contents just abandoned, strewn across the rooms. Mike and I walked respectfully around the 46 steam occupants, noting their demise. The Tremeloes may have thought that 'Silence is golden', but this was the silence of the dead. As we walked down one of the running roads (was that an appropriate term in the circumstances?), we heard the groan of tired bearings, as WD 90615, still warm and alive, dragged 42149, 45647 and 90650 to join the other members of the undead. Like some kind of voyeurs, from behind a line of dead locomotives we watched the uncoupling of these latest fatalities. It transpired that Healey Mills depot had opened in May, and Wakefield shed, redundant with the new pattern of working, had been abandoned overnight, along with all its residents. Mike and I crept out of this one time home of giants, but now the haunt of ghosts, and drove off in search of signs of life. Fortunately, Royston shed provided evidence of this, in the form of 26 8Fs, mostly in steam, before we continued west to Low Moor depot. There were 19 steamers here, but a number were in store. No less than twelve Stanier 2-6-4 tanks adorned the shed yard, along with B1 61306, an ex Hull stalwart, and classmate 61388. We dropped in on the Keighley and Worth Valley Railway to observe its progress, before retracing our tracks eastward. No steam was evident at Mirfield, Manningham or Stourton, for all had shut to steam in January. Surprisingly, we didn't drop in on Holbeck, but we did sample the limited pleasures of a very much dieselised Neville Hill MPD, which took the form of 3442 'The Great Marquess'. Our faces must have been 'A whiter shade of pale' as we journeyed home, knowing that time was fast running out for steam. But this was no time to get too downhearted, for there was always one more trip.

Standard 4-6-0 73141, from Patricroft, must have taken a fancy to the East Coast, for it hauled the trip 1H92 through Hull the first two Saturdays in July. Two events of great importance took place on the second Saturday. Firstly, it was the final weekend of Southern Region steam operation. The Kinks song 'Waterloo Sunset', which charted at the time, conjures up the wonderful picture of a gentle whiff of steam drifting across the Thames, with the ultimate suburban train leaving the terminus for the last time behind a Standard tank, with the setting summer sun glistening on the river. Secondly, Brian and I performed our first concert together. Riley High School was to have an evening of folk music, amazingly, on Saturday July 8th. We sang 'Puff, the magic dragon' and 'Where have all the flowers gone?', accompanying ourselves on the guitar. Mercifully, my world was now focussing more on music, and that helped ease the pain of the passing of steam, but I still wondered 'Where have all the steam engines gone?'.

Not that I had written my beloved steamers off yet, far from it, for Mike and I were off to the Midlands on Sunday July 16th. We were trying to kill several birds with one stone. Our first port of call was to be Westhouses, 16G, for there'd been reports of steam working at Williamthorpe Colliery, near Chesterfield, and these turned out to be true, for we found three 'Jinties', 47289, 47313 and 47534 on the shed. 47289 was having its buffers riveted, and we were told that fellow loco, 47383, along with 68012, were up at the colliery. Apparently, 68006 was being dismantled at Buxton shed to provide spares for 68012. This was most gratifying, and gave us heart as we headed south, and further into a steam free zone. Tyseley was still home to nine steamers, including two G.W.R relics, pannier 1638, and Castle 7029 'Clun Castle'. The rest were 'Black Fives' or Standard 5 4-6-0s, down from the North West for tyre turning. As expected, Stourbridge was a blank, but at least it was worth a try as we headed onwards to the Severn Valley Railway. Ivatt 2-6-0 46443 and 0-6-0 3205, which I copped, were in steam on that summer afternoon. Mike and I then decided to return north via more steamy climes. On the way, we dropped in at Oxley shed, which was home to ten defunct steamers, with all but 8F 48492 stored outside, before striking out for Stoke. 44 locos were on the depot that sunny day, but this figure was totally eclipsed by the 82 engines littered around Crewe South's large yard. 'Duke of Gloucester' was still there, as was its tiny companion, 'Jinty' 47566, plus four Britannias. Drifting homeward, Northwich shed beckoned, with 33 locos, mostly 8Fs, slumbering in the haze of the yard. 48735 was to be my penultimate cop, having escaped me for so many years and shed visits. The last call of the day was on an old favourite, Stockport Edgeley. It was now evening, and Mike and I took time to rest for a short while on the scrub land at the south end of the depot, for it was still light. The summer was in full swing, and my love of steam was still undiminished, but as I looked over the smoke drifting out of the shed vents, I knew that I wouldn't see another summer like it.

The following Saturday, I made the reckless decision to leave Hull at 13.34, to travel deep into enemy territory! I needed one last loco - B1 61138, which was in Departmental Service as No. 26. As I sped south, I noted that Retford G.N. shed was still intact, but the tracks had been removed. It was the first, and last time that I did March shed, and fortunately, the B1 was there. I have stated that Salisbury was the last steam shed that I needed to bash, but as March had closed to steam in December 1963, I didn't really count that in the equation! Not that steam stopped visiting the town after that date, for I remember that Mike dropped in there in February 1965 and reported to me that the shed was alive with steam. Apparently, engines visiting Whitemoor Yard from the East Midlands could no longer be serviced at New England shed, for it had shut in January, and so stayed in town! The B1 that I needed had been allocated to Norwich, but I'd got wind that it was to be found at March. It was then a long journey home, but after July 22nd 1967, I no longer needed any engine numbers of steam engines in service.

I hadn't done badly though, for in five years I'd seen over 5400 different steam engines, of which 523 were WDs, 609 8Fs, and no fewer than 716 'Black Fives'! Additionally, I had only missed 17 9Fs, 29 Bulleid light pacifics, and just 3 Merchant Navy pacifics, which is pretty amazing when you consider how far the Southern Region was from Hull! Unfortunately, because of my late start to trainspotting, the only class that I completed in its entirety was the Britannias. Not that any of this prevented me from going on more trainspotting journeys, it's just that I didn't really spot trains anymore! Furthermore, I'd managed to visit 157 different depots; some of them on a number of occasions. By the end of steam in August 1968, when I was still only 16, I had done no less than 500 shed bashes. This final tally didn't include my local depot, Dairycoates!

At the end of the school year, having risen from the B stream the year before, I finished 4th place in 4A, and that pleased my form tutor. I'd really got into cycling by this time, and the first day of the school holidays found my friend George and I biking all the way to Ravenscar. We then set off home into a head wind, which knocked the stuffing out of us. We made it home, and we did do another long trip later in the year, but train trips definitely looked a more attractive proposition to me. Mike obliged, with a run out to Williamthorpe Colliery on Wednesday August 2nd to watch 47289 and 68012 shunting the sidings there. Better was to follow, for on the following Saturday, we were off to tape record the last workings on the former Hull and Barnsley Railway at Pickburn Colliery and Wrangbrook Junction, and on the day, 8F 48537 was to do the honours. The one thing I do remember about the day was that I overslept, and in the rush to get ready, I put on odd boots! I hoped that no one would notice, for most people would have considered me mad anyway for chasing steam engines around the country. We also took time to bash Royston depot, with twenty 8Fs on, and Normanton, home to 32 locos. Thirteen were WDs, but there were a few Stanier tanks and 'Coffee Pots', and Standard 4-6-0 73159 was visiting from Patricroft. 49 dead locomotives graced Wakefield shed, the most noteworthy of which were Standards 77002 and 77012.

It was now high summer, and steam excursions still made it through Hull to the coast. I noted 'Black Five' 44662 on Saturday August 12th, and it was to be a regular on the Bradford to Bridlington run that summer. I spent a great deal of time round at Mikes, but I still saw a lot of Dave, one of the original Anlaby Road regulars from 1963. He was due to go to University in the autumn, and he would then slip out of my orbit, once and for all. A new friend appeared at his time, Simon. He was younger, and had only recently caught the trainspotting bug. I felt like an old hand compared to him, but he was to accompany me on some of the last trips that I ever took in search of steam. One final fling was needed, and fortunately, my mam obliged, for she paid for a Northern Railrover for me. I was in search of steam haulage, wherever I could find it. It all started off in a low key fashion with a visit to Holbeck shed on Sunday 13th. There were 29 engines on shed, with 45562 'Alberta' and 'Black Five' 45428 bulled up for their summer duties. Also present were Britannia 70021 'Morning Star' and preserved Midland Railway 2-4-0, number 158A. I had noticed K1 62012 and Q6 63366 at Selby, obviously on their way to Hull for breaking. I then visited Dairycoates, and here is a complete register of the dead locos present: 42954, 43011, 43077, 44666, 44989, 45033, 45079, 45094, 45383, 45441, 45446, 48029, 48075, 48123, 48126, 48159, 48185, 48221, 48502, 48738, 62001, 62065, 90429, 90655, 92006, and 92150. This will give you some idea of the variety of engines that made Draper's of Hull their last resting place.

The real excitement started on the Monday, when I left Hull at 06.00, bound for Manchester and Preston. There was still plenty of steam to be seen, and I noted nearly thirty at work on the way. Britannia 70013 'Oliver Cromwell' was noted in ex-works condition at Preston, heading south with a mixed train of freight, coaches and dead DMUs! This Britannia was a celebrity, for it had been the very last steam locomotive to be overhauled by B.R., leaving the works at Crewe in February. My first taste of steam haulage was behind 44964 on the 11.58 to Blackpool, where I took the opportunity to partake of the delights of the North shed. The depot was home to 44727, 45038, 45215, 48386, 48491 and 48636. I then headed home, regaining steam haulage at Preston, with 45347 hauling the 15.45 to Manchester. Even at this very late juncture, it was still quite common to see steam hauled freights in the vicinity of Leeds station, and WD 90430 did me the honours that day.

The next day turned out even better, for I headed off to Hellifield, where a glimpse in the old shed revealed 44027, 'Thundersley', 42700, V2 4771, L.N.W.R. No. 1439 and G.E.R. No. 1217, which was a cop for me. I then wandered back to the station to decide what to do next. Just then, a Long Meg freight pulled in behind 9F 92125. Cheekily, I asked the guard if there was any chance of a brakevan ride to Blackburn. 'No chance', came the reply, and disappointed, I ambled off down the platform. The signal came off for the goods, and I heard the wagons clanking as they gathered speed past me. The next thing I knew, the guard had grabbed my arm and pulled me onto the veranda of his van! He quickly drew me into the vehicle, to avoid the gaze of the signalman, and I was off on the brakevan ride of my life. 8F 48445 banked us up the Whalley incline, and too soon I was dumped off unceremoniously at Blackburn station just after one in the afternoon. The guard and the train carried on as if nothing had happened, and I sat down to eat my lunch. Where to now, I thought? Preston beckoned once more, and 45331 was to be the motive power for the 15.45 to Manchester that day.

The following morning I got up late, and I arrived in Leeds City just in time to catch the 09.58 excursion to Belle Vue, hauled by 44896. Having a rover ticket gave me great flexibility, and I could just follow any whim that pleased me. After alighting at Belle Vue, I made my way to Manchester Victoria, and Preston, in order to sample the 15.45 back to Manchester again, which was hauled by 44713 that day. Thursday found me bashing Carnforth shed, which had 46 locos in residence. Many were now stored, even Britannia 70027 'Rising Star'. I then spent a pleasant hour on the station before catching the Euston train, which left at 11.39 behind 44872. On the train I met a Scottish enthusiast who got me up to speed with events north of the border. He mentioned a soda ash train that he believed was still occasionally steam hauled as far as Larbert. At Preston I caught a late running Blackpool train, which had unusual motive power in the form of 'Coffee Pot' 43004. Once again, I travelled back to Manchester on the 15.45, this time behind 45450. On Friday, I had a jaunt out to Liverpool with Brian, ostensibly to look around The Cavern and some of The Beatles old haunts, for Brian was a huge Beatles fan. Unfortunately for us, that was the one day that week that the heavens opened, and that put a damper on the whole outing.

The last day of my rover ticket, Saturday, was sunny though, and I made the most of it, for I travelled to Bradford Exchange in order to experience the greatest show in town. That is, the sight of two steam hauled passenger trains scheduled to leave the terminus at the same time, 08.20. One departure was to Bridlington, hauled by 44800, and I travelled on it as far as Normanton, and the other train was to Poole, with 61306 in charge. What a spectacle they made as they left, with cameras snapping to the left and to the right as they stormed out of town. However, within a month the show was over, and this awesome sight had been consigned to history. At Normanton, I dashed around the shed, home to 27 steamers, and noted 90615 hauling 90236 and 90654 through the station. I then set off for Leeds. Jubilee 45562 'Alberta' was on the 10.17 Carlisle train, and I was off to the north behind it.

There was still plenty of steam at work over the Settle and Carlisle, and at the border town, I leapt onto the first southbound steam hauled train, which happened to be Manchester bound behind 45295. It left late, and suffered further delays near Penrith. It then made a brave attempt to make up for the late running with a display of pyrotechnics, and speeds into the nineties. I believe the run is recorded in a copy of 'The Railway Magazine' somewhere. I met up with my Scottish friend once again, and compared notes on the week's activities, steam wise, that is. The train was full of fellow enthusiasts who wanted to make hay while the sun shone in that long summer of love. Everyone knew it was the last full summer of steam, and there would never be another one like it. With one spirit, we were all there for the steam, the assault on the senses, the buzz. All of us were travelling, packed into every vestibule corner and any available window, to mark our place in time, and in years to come, to say to a less fortunate generation, 'I was there!' The West Coast mainline was still crammed full of steam power, and at Preston I managed a negative connection, for I swapped platforms to catch a train that should have left two minutes before we were due in! I was now heading north at 15.33 behind 44873, on a Windermere train. Changing trains, and direction, at Oxenholme, I headed south again behind Britannia 70051 'Firth of Forth', before alighting at Preston and heading home. So that frantic last day on my Northern Railrover ended. Yes, you can sing with The Beatles 'Baby you're a rich man' indeed, if you enjoy a few days in your life like those in August 1967.

Chapter 23

Hello, goodbye

I now come to the chapter that I've long dreaded to write - the last twelve months of steam in Britain. My journey has started out over five years before, and I'd run the race the best that any youngster could. I remember in June watching The Beatles perform 'All you need is love', live on the first ever world wide T.V. satellite link up. Unfortunately for me, love wasn't enough, for the relentless passage of time was ultimately to seal my trainspotting days. Additionally, I needed money to chase the steam dragons, and the prospect of employment was still several years in front of me. Luckily for me, my new passion, music, was to help fill some of the gap left by the demise of the steam engine.

Not that my railway days were quite over in August 1967, for no sooner had I finished my Northern Rover, than our family was off to Birkenhead on the 25th, for my dad's ship was now berthed there. While staying there, the news came through that Brian Epstein was dead. For Beatles fans, that was a shock of seismic proportions, for he was the man behind their initial fame. It really did mark the beginning of the end for the Fab Four, but on the steam scene, it was now definitely well into the end game. Even though I no longer needed to chase cops, I still kept a careful log of the locomotives that I saw on my travels, and there was still much to see. Even opposite Neville Hill depot, I recorded 45080 of Holbeck, and 92152 of Birkenhead, ready to take up freights. We returned on the 30th, and my trusty logbook records Britannia 70004 'William Shakespeare' shunting near Manchester Victoria, and Stanier tank 42251, 'in excellent condition' at Leeds City station.

Mike was keen to record for posterity the final workings of pre-grouping steam in County Durham. Therefore, we set off from Hull on the evening of Wednesday September 6th in ODT 709, bound for Newcastle. We stayed at his uncle's that night, and the following morning we drove down to Ryhope Junction. It goes without saying that it was a gloriously sunny day. The anthem for the day was 'Pleasant Valley Sunday' by The Monkees, which was playing on a radio at a filling station as Mike bought petrol.

Nice sentiments, wrong day though. The central characters in the drama were to be 63395, 65811 and 65894, which fussed backwards and forwards, doing what they'd done for countless years. We also visited the Silksworth Colliery branch, to watch 65811 wrench no less than 26 loaded wagons up the severe incline, in a volcanic explosion of smoke and steam. We then returned to our vantage point at Ryhope. It must have been coincidence, but two of the three locos we noted that day were to survive into preservation. I have always been a fan of WD 2-8-0s, and was greatly saddened that one of the B.R. examples wasn't saved from the cutter's torch. In Hull they were known as 'Dub-dees', but up north they were always called 'Clankies', because of the clank from their valve gear when they were on overrun. I can still clearly remember hearing the sound of one, which turned out to be 90382, drifting towards us that warm September morning. Within two weeks, as far as County Durham was concerned, that sound belonged to the history books. I also remember the journey home, for Mike was flogging the Austin Somerset mercilessly down the A1, as he always did, when he was stopped by the police. They didn't like the condition that the car appeared to be in, and frankly, neither did I. Mike had to produce his documents in Hull the following day, and I think that he got off so lightly only because he was giving his mother a lift back from his uncle's. The fact that he bought cheap lubricating oil by the gallon from the local bargain shop Boyes, and then used the tins to pop rivet the bodywork will give you an idea of the state of his car!

Not that this little episode stopped our shenanigans, for Mike and I were off to Cumbria the following weekend. The Association of Railway Preservation Societies was holding their A.G.M. at Ravenglass, and Mike, as an observer member intended to be there. We left Hull on Saturday 9th at 08.00, and rattled across to the Ravenglass & Eskdale Railway. After the meeting, we camped next to the railway at Seascale. On Sunday, we dropped in on the 22 locos slumbering on Workington shed. No less than twelve were 'Coffee Pots', and even at this late date there were still interesting workings, for 8Fs 48304 and 48735 were from Northwich, and had worked north on silica trains bound for Whitehaven. Our journey home took us via Bishop Auckland, where we watched 4472 'Flying Scotsman' on a north bound excursion, and more interestingly, 7029 'Clun Castle' storming south at Tollerton with another special.

As an interlude to playing my guitar, I took time out on Saturday September 16th to cycle no less than 126 miles with my mate George. We covered most of the Wolds up to Malton, before returning via Sledmere, Driffield and Aldbrough. There were no contrary winds to hinder us, and my bottom survived to cycle another day! By this time, Mike had moved to James Reckitt Avenue, and so my bicycle was essential to visit him. He was now becoming more heavily involved in the preservation movement, with his eyes on an ex-H.B.R. coach at Springhead Works. Ultimately, he was able to save the vehicle, and I occasionally gave him a hand with it, sometimes helped by my new found spotting pal, Simon. Another character who appeared on the railway horizon at this time was Paddy Goss. He was at Hull University, and was to be instrumental in saving ex-Port Talbot Railway loco, G.W.R. no 813. He and Mike used to spend hours conjuring up fund raising schemes, interspersed with arguments about politics, on which they were diametrically opposed!

Dairycoates was not neglected, for Mike and I visited together on October 1st. On shed were 43096, 61019, 90061, 90116, 90200, 90230, 90309, 90321, 90339, 90388, 90434, 90459, 90698, 92006 and 92150, which were to be joined a week later by 42052, 42196, 42233 and 42699. Plenty of engines were still being drawn to Hull, but none were in steam. Our next trip was on November 25th to follow 60019 'Bittern' on a run out. We saw it at Skipton, Gargarve, and a little later at Euxton. The Who might have been able to 'See for miles', but it was the autumn of the terrible foot and mouth outbreak, and while we waited for the special next to the West Coast mainline, all we could see was the smoke rising from burning carcasses! Mike and I were then off to a Hull F.C. versus Oldham match, before catching up with 60019 once more, running an hour late, at Mirfield station at 19.33. The following day, my dad kindly took Simon and I to Haworth to see how the Keighley and Worth Valley Railway was progressing. On the way back, I visited Holbeck depot, that old favourite, one last time. In the roundhouse, out of steam, were five engines, 42251, 42616, 44854, 45428 and 62005. I had suspected that steam was about to finish in the West Riding, but this visit confirmed that suspicion. At least two of the residents were subsequently to be preserved, but at that moment, the sound of steam drew Simon and I to the shed entrance. There, under Nineveh Street Bridge, was a very much alive Britannia, number 70024 'Vulcan'. We were to watch it leave Leeds shortly afterwards with a northbound parcels train.

By the end of November, condemned locomotives were no longer stabled at Dairycoates prior to dispatch to Draper's yard. Instead, they were sent directly to his new site at Neptune Street, for he had now abandoned the Sculcoates yard. On Sunday December 3rd, Mike and I recorded for posterity 44808, 46515, 48548, 61019, 61123, 61189, 78007, 90210, 90233, 90321 and 92211. It may have been trainspotting, but it felt more like picking over the bones of the deceased. Fortunately, I had other interests to divert my mind from those depressing final months, for the following week, I got my first electric guitar! But shed bashing wasn't dead yet, for to Simon, it was still a new game. So on Saturday December 16th, travelling via Newcastle, we headed to Carlisle on a football excursion. We saw no steam at all until Citadel station, but then made up for that deficiency by a visit to Workington. There were 15 residents, 11 of which were 'Coffee Pots', but only two locos were in steam, 45294 and 45411. It was then back to Carlisle and Kingmoor depot. Like so many spotters before, but few after that date, we caught the St. Anns bus from English Street and descended on this special place. There were 80 steamers on shed, including 18 Britannias, but the majority of engines were in store. It was then a race back to town, and Upperby shed. It was home to just six locos, which included Crewe Works last outshopped steam engine, Britannia 70013 'Oliver Cromwell' in excellent condition. To Simon it was all new and wonderful, and that was good, but I knew it was over, and even the sight of 60019 'Bittern' on York shed couldn't bring any cheer to the winter night. Not that I rested on my laurels, for the following day, my dad drove me to Goole, and patiently waited in the car as I paid my last respects to the 11 WDs stored there, waiting in limbo for their final call.

But that wasn't to be the last outing of the year. I might have got rock and roll, but while there were still steam engines to chase, I was off. This time, it was to be to the Crewe and Manchester areas. The earliest sign of steam had been at Bradley Junction, near Huddersfield, with the sighting of 8F 48433 on an east bound freight. However, once again something must have gone wrong, for after Northwich shed, and its 13 inhabitants, Simon and I headed north, not south, from Hartford station. This brought us to Speke Junction, home to 42 steamers, mostly stored. On Edge Hill we noted 51 locos in the weak winter sun, and many were still in steam. We then crossed the Mersey, only to find Birkenhead depot completely bare. According to a railway worker, 'Black Five' 45305, which was ultimately saved by Draper's, had visited the shed fifteen minutes earlier, but we were too late, too late indeed. Our last call was at Newton Heath, home to 55 engines, mostly in steam. Ironically, it was pitch black as we travelled out to Dean Lane, and my mind ran back four years exactly to the Bolton shedbash that didn't happen, because 'it was too dark'. I was giving Simon none of that nonsense, for it was now or never. Incidentally, Simon's dad worked in Paragon house, and so he was travelling on privilege tickets, but I wasn't, and that final trip of 1967 cost me no less than 57/1!

Love Affair had their 'Everlasting love', and I had mine, but it was painful to watch the decline of steam in the final months. Therefore, as 1967 became 1968, more of my energies went into the guitar, amplification, and building primitive effects pedals. Mike and I still visited Neptune Street, noting 90016, 90057, 90094, 90099, 90262, 90427, 90670 and 90688 there on January 7th. They were joined on the 28th by 42141, 42689, 48703, 48721 and 92205. Simon and I sometimes spent time down at Springhead Works with Mike on the H&BR coach that he'd secured for posterity, but I needed another trip to spice up Simon's interest in trains. The Beatles might have had 'Lady Madonna', but we had a ticket to the North West on March 16th. We started at Patricroft, home to 34 locos, including stored Britannia 70012 'John of Gaunt', but at least most were in steam, before bashing Newton Heath once more. Classmate 70023 'Venus' was stored there, but most of the other 40 residents were still alive. Bolton yielded 30 engines, and Lostock Hall 31 more, before we headed to the final shed of the day, Carnforth. 10A was home to 36 steamers, including 70021 'Morning Star' on the scrapline. The day was bitterly cold, and as I was feeling quite ill, I was glad to get home. However, we had seen 200 steam locomotives that day, and Simon had enjoyed himself. There weren't that many steamers left, and he didn't have to travel to cop them, for most of them were heading towards him! At the end of March we noted 42093, 42251, 42252, 42616, 44861, 45092, 45377, 48074, 48559, 90430, 90605, 90699 and 90721 at Neptune Street. On April 6th Simon and I went to Cottingham to watch 4472 'Flying Scotsman' on one of its many trips out.

As much as I was getting into music, I still felt the need to chase steam while there was still any to chase. Therefore, on Saturday April 20th, I set out alone, with the intention of bashing as many of the remaining steam depots that I could. I saw no steam until I noted 48549 at Guide Bridge. Heaton Mersey was home to 28 engines, nearly all 8Fs, with many in steam. For the final time, I walked into Stockport Edgeley shed and recorded just 13 locos, mostly 'Black Fives', and mostly in steam. It was then off to Crewe, for word had not reached me yet that the shed had closed to steam the previous November. On shed was A4 4468 'Mallard', but no other steam locomotives were present. On leaving the depot, disaster struck, for a railway policeman had watched me bash the shed, and was out to catch me. I ran back down Gresty Lane, but his car soon overtook me. It was exactly three years since I'd been nabbed at Dairycoates, and I had no intention of ending my trainspotting career with another prosecution. Fortunately, I told him a sob story and the policeman took pity on me, but I decided to abandon the outing and get home while I was still ahead.

Mike's Austin Somerset had finally given up the ghost, and in its place he'd bought a grey A35 van. On June 29th, we headed off to the Keighley and Worth Valley Railway to tape record some live steam there, in the shape of U.S.A. tank 30072 and Ivatt 2-6-2 tank 41241. The Kinks released their nostalgic song 'Days', which certainly captured the mood, but Mike and I, like Canned Heat were 'On the road again' for two last trips. On August 2nd, to chronicle the passing of the age, we set foot in Rose Grove for the last time. On the way, we'd dropped in at Wakefield depot for old time's sake, and observed 44912 stored there. After noting 45156 on a cement train at Whalley, we drove over to Lostock Hall, home to 38 locos. Naturally, Carnforth shed was to be our last port of call, but after noting 20 numbers, we were evicted by the shed foreman, who must have been beyond himself by this time. My final shed bash, and I was thrown out, the ignominy of it!

The Beach Boys reached number one in August with 'Do it again', and I would dearly have loved to start all over again, and watch all those lovely steam locomotives once more, but that was not to be. The date was August 11th 1968, a date seared into the minds of railway enthusiasts. Mike and I, like many others, paid our final respects by visiting the Settle and Carlisle line that day to watch Britannia 70013 'Oliver Cromwell' heading north on the 'Fifteen

Guinea Special', run to commemorate the end of steam traction. Later in the day, we saw 44781 and 44871 taking on water at Blea Moor, while double heading the train south. Mike and I were in no hurry to get home, and we stayed on the hills long enough to watch, twenty minutes later, the Britannia running light engine in the direction of the special. We watched the final trace of steam disappear as it threaded its way south, into preservation and into the history books. Mike's mind was now to focus more on preservation, and mine on my G.C.E. results, which were to be released on the 26th. However, we both now had a moment to reflect on the sentiments of the song that was to make Mary Hopkins a household name when it reached the top spot on September 4th, 'Those were the days'. Yes, those were the days, and thousands of trainspotters would have agreed wholeheartedly with that statement, for the like of those days would never be seen again. On August 30th, The Beatles released 'Hey Jude', backed by 'Revolution'. Twenty thousand steam locomotives to none in little over ten years, that was nothing short of a revolution. Looking back now, do I miss steam engines and the thrill of the chase? Yes, of course I do! Do I miss the excitement of the 60's music scene, and the incredible phenomenon that was The Beatles? Most certainly, but after the passage of four decades, what I miss most of all is my youth.

Printed in the United Kingdom
by Lightning Source UK Ltd.
128025UK00001B/1-105/A